Think Snow

by Kenneth Kinsler

First published by CreateSpace in May 2015.

ISBN- 13: 978-1500299002

ISBN- 10: 1500299006

Library of Congress number: LCCN# 2014919662

The snowflake image is a trademark of Ken Kinsler

Printed in the USA

Table of Contents:

Foreword
by David J. Kinsler

Normally, a book's "foreword" is a slight introduction into the bloodstream of the heart of a book's topic of conversation. Unfortunately, this won't work - not this time. Although I'm the birth son of the author, there's no conceivable way I can attempt to initiate or imitate the heartbeat of my father's words, his experiences, or his alter-reality as a drafted United States Army Soldier during one of the ugliest years of the Vietnam War in 1968.

What I can speak of is that it wasn't until after reading his first draft in 2014, that I was finally able to acquire the missing jigsaw pieces to a puzzle I've been scrambling to assemble since I was a little grommet. I was lucky enough to grow up in a house filled with love, respect, discipline, family dinner time, and long days surfing the waves in New Smyrna Beach, Florida. As a little boy, I was extremely interested in my daddy's identity and his duties within the persona of a soldier - always wondering what it was like to "be" in a war. Silly rabbit, after consuming this book I now realize what I was truly searching for - an empathic understanding of what it's like for the "war" to "be" in my dad.

In June of 1993, I was finally of age and able to purchase a cocktail in a bar (even though I never did). I was a "retired" competitive surfer who was about to enter his senior year of undergraduate school and take over the world of advertising and publicity with a crisp Bachelor of Arts degree. My parents still lived in New Smyrna Beach, but my father was commuting to Miami every week, working as a foreman, reconstructing the Kendall area (which was devastated by the vicious, son of a bitch Hurricane Andrew). My father brought me on the job as a day laborer to make some sweet cash during summer break. We lived in a mobile home with a cranky, alcoholic biker who had a short wick on his temper. We referred to our living quarters as our "temporary tour bus" and it nestled refuge on the front lawn of an Asian American's home.

During the reconstruction of the suburban area that was affected, it was common to see a block party of construction workers walking the street late at night. Sometimes they were screaming at the cars on the nearby I-95 Interstate, but really we were all watching out for drive-by looters who were searching for materials and on-site tools to steal and cash in for their quick heroin fix.

One night after my dad and I washed-up, we hit a McDonalds to inhale a couple of Big Macs. After we finished feasting on fatty acids and fries, we made our exit through the "Golden Arches" and began the short journey to the work truck in the parking lot. As we approached the pick-up, my father suddenly stopped, and with a clinched fist and an extended arm, he slowly moved in front of me and pushed me backwards.

I almost stumbled while looking at him because I saw the grimace and facial intensity of a human, not known to be my father. Within a mere 1.2 seconds, I watched my calm, collected, relatively happy father go somewhere mentally and physically. Every muscle in his chest, neck, and forearms began to bulge. He stopped breathing. He literally transferred his memories of emotional behavioral skills of the past into the present. He was a soldier, in Vietnam, all over again. He turned into a killing machine before my naive eyes. Almost in slow motion, I began to look forward as a visual came into focus of about five young, angry looking and very desperate gangbangers who were looking to steal our truck or equipment. They were surrounding our truck's bed, eyeing the lock to the back which contained maybe $20,000.00 worth of equipment. Nobody flashed a gun, even though we knew they had one. Nobody greeted us with an ultimatum. The alpha-banger, maybe in his late 20's, took one step toward my dad and me, stopping maybe seven feet in front of us before he froze in his tracks. His gang decided to slowly creep forward behind him, rallying around their leader. My dad opened his mouth and shouted, "Come On! Come On, you motherfuckers! I've killed before, and I'll kill again! You wanna die, motherfuckers?" And with that introduction and the fierce tone of "No Fear" in my father's voice, they very slowly backed-up and retreated. Never did they stop looking at us as they walked backwards and cowered back to the slum where they came from.

Before I could even come to my senses and process what had just happened, my father told me to get into the truck and lock the doors. What happened next was even more eerie.

My father stood behind the truck for a moment - alone. Then he began to pace around the back of the truck for a few minutes. I wasn't sure if he was waiting for them to return, or if he actually wanted the gang back in his face. Maybe he was just allowing the internal demons that came back to haunt him a shallow exit strategy before he sat next to me in the Ford 250 king cab. Then, after I spent a few moments (which seemed like an hour) of suffering tachycardia and whispering, "Holy Shit... Holy Shit... Holy..." he joined me in the cab.

He took a deep breath, and very quietly whispered, "Don't tell your mother what just happened." I listened to him. I never spoke of that event until years later with some close college buddies over a few Coca-Colas.

It was that summer of 1993 when I began to truly realize the unfortunate truth that my father had spirits inside his soul that were running like wild horses on a big farm. "The Devil in the Details" within my father, showed their face on that hot, muggy Miami night. And to see the face, the actual face of horror and death of the devil within, is one of the scariest moments you'll ever experience as a human. This is especially true when the person consumed reflects back to a former life to protect his own son's life, his life, and transforms into a killing machine - ready to die to protect his family at all costs. I'm not sure if my dad even remembers the events that took place that night. Whether he just downloaded the event into his mental "Dropbox" or deleted it from his cognitive hard drive, it still haunts me to know that he would have died for me, his little David, that night. Nevertheless, he could never erase what kind of impression it left with me, his son. I never felt safer or more secure. I was never more proud of my humble and hard-working father. He saved my life that night.

Later that summer during our weekly 4-hour drive(s) back north to New Smyrna Beach, my father began to slowly open up about his tour of duty in Vietnam. It was the first time he ever told me a few stories, all PG-13 granted, but he started to trust me. He began to laugh and giggle about the trickery and genius of his earlier enemy - some guy(s) named "Charlie." It was then, during that summer break, that I realized my dad wasn't really free of his chains. No matter how many evangelical mega-maniacs prayed over him, casted out spirits, or verbally tried to relate with him over a $2 coffee and pound cake, my father was incapable of allowing his guilt to fly away on the wings of a prayer.

When my father's soul mate and wife of 38 years, my mother, passed away, my father began to actually sit down with a mental health specialist at his V.A. clinic. Over the first year, I began to hear a unique and foreign tone in my father's voice. It was happiness, with a side of anticipation. He actually told me that he was enjoying his time in therapy; not at first, but as the therapist began to take a keen interest in my dad's behaviors, thought patterns, and systematic values, he was becoming transparent and more honest than ever before. Not with me, not with my sister, but more importantly, with himself.

He never disclosed his progress to us over the airwaves via cell phone, but he began to start writing. It was in this fashion that my dad disclosed to me that he was contemplating writing a book. Over the next 3 years, my father went a little "MIA" on me and our family, but in a healthy way. Because when my dad is determined to accomplish a task, create a piece of art, or rehabilitate someone's living room, he's not leaving until it's done. And that's what he did - he wrote a book.

It's more of a conversation piece; and when reading it, you'll almost feel like you're just sitting at Starbucks with a coffee while listening to someone (with no filter) describing how it was to be drafted into the jungle. That's my dad. He's the most approachable, friendly, and engaging guy on the coffee shop's stoop - and he's saved all those conversations, stories, feelings, experiences, questions, and pain he suffered as a soldier in Nam, for you, the reader. The stranger. The baby boomer. The Gen-X'er. The Hipster. The senior citizen who lost their son in that ugly war. He wrote this book for you - and for his own personal therapy.

In closing, one of my most respected friends, Richard Patrick, started the rock band, Filter, right after I graduated college. He's taken his band to play for the active military in Iraq, Afghanistan, Kuwait and other middle-eastern regions multiple times over the past 6 years - sometimes on his own dime - and I respect the hell out of him for it. We've engaged in intense conversations on topics of the current war, the horror stories he's been told by military fans, my experience feeling inept as a soldier's son, and the lack of respect or ignorance some of our closest neighbors have regarding the Veterans of today and yesterday.

Whether our family or friends have seen combat last week or nearly 40 years ago, the memories and pain still linger within those who served and survived. In 2008, Patrick (and Filter) released an album, "Anthems for the Damned." The album included a single "Soldiers of Misfortune" which was marketed to rock stations around the country.

The entire album was a tribute to the men and women of the United States Military and to one of his close friends who died in Iraq – just within weeks after arriving.

Sometimes I've wished I could've performed a song, or a theatrical dedication to my father for his sacrifice and the pride I feel within. I've always desired to publicly express my love and respect for what he was called to do for this beautiful country.

Then, ironically, while recently working on a project in Los Angeles with Patrick and his band, my father gave me a call while I was directing a music video. He mentioned that he'd like me to take a shot at writing the foreword for this book (but only if I felt inclined). My eyes swelled with tears. My heart dropped and my dream came true. Although my words in this foreword of my father's book may not be as cool as a rock song, it finally happened. I got my shot at telling the world how proud I am to be the son of a GRUNT.

I'm the son of a man who sacrificed his life for his country and fellow soldiers - and lived to tell the story. I'm the son of a man, who was (and still is) my greatest superhero. Hopefully after reading this foreword, you've heard a catchy riff, or a chord progression that you can't get out of your head – if so, just wait until you hear the harmonies and melodies of my father's experience in Vietnam. So here's my chance to preface and present the biggest and coolest rock star in my life, "My Father."

I hope you're ready. I hope you clear your mechanism. All I can say now is, "**Be Prepared**."

Be Prepared to learn how much fun it was to enter boot camp after being drafted at the "ripe" age of 26.

Be Prepared to feel the pain and anger of what it's like to leave your friends, your family, your loved ones, and have your identity stripped away.

Be Prepared to feel what it's like to kill another human being.

Be Prepared to learn why it was so important to stuff your pants into your Army issued combat boots.

Be Prepared to learn how to "de-sensitize" your thoughts, morals, and central nervous system.

Be Prepared to identify what it was like to put your life in the arms, the eyes, the senses, and the experience of a "green" point man who just turned 18.

Be Prepared to hear a new perspective on what racism was truly like in the jungle - thousands of miles away from the protests at the United States Capital or on the grass at Kent State University.

Be Prepared to attempt to understand why it was more important to "react" in the jungle than actually "think."

Be Prepared to hear from a decorated soldier what the "Battle of HILL 684" was really like - and the reactions you received when other soldiers saw it written on your helmet.

Be Prepared to find out how much fun it was to drink warm Budweiser and Jack Daniels - with a side order of malaria.

Be Prepared to redefine what true horror actually is.

Be Prepared to learn how to get murdered, by your own Platoon.

Be Prepared to hear why it was so important to take the lessons your parents taught you as a little boy with you into the jungle.

Be Prepared to learn what it was like to walk into the TET Offensive on day one.

Be Prepared to hear why and how a soldier could look a Catholic Priest in the face and yell, "Fuck You!"

Be Prepared to learn how "True Love" can actually save your life.

Be Prepared to understand why it's so important, to just sometimes, "Think Snow."

Editor's Preface
by Sean Donovan

When Ken Kinsler first shared his idea to write this book with me I was immediately stoked for him - and honored to be part of the process. I've always had a love for writing and collaborating with other authors. My love of writing stems from the fact that I believe that the mere thought of writing a book begins a cathartic process between the mind and soul from deep within the author.

Good writing is the crystallization of pure thought. Publishing a book allows us to share our "crystals" with the world. The release of ideas, thoughts, dreams and real-life experiences through the art of writing is very fulfilling and even healing for some; for others, it's all about learning from the wisdom and experiences of others or maybe just taking an adventurous journey through the eyes of another. Either way, writing is an age-old practice that has been utilized and passed down by generations – in fact, most of history has been relayed by the written word. The word "history" is derived from "his story."

I could feel the excitement in Kinsler's eyes as we sat and discussed his plans for this book. He lit up with enthusiasm as he recounted some of the experiences he would later share in this book. It was no secret that Kinsler had a burning desire within himself to write about his innermost feelings and even release some demons that he had harbored for over 40 years. Just the thought and discussion of writing this book had already started to free him from the metaphorical shackles that had held him hostage for so many years.

What really impressed me the most during our initial meeting was Kinsler's genuine desire to help others with their struggles through his writing. Whether you're a veteran who is struggling with post-traumatic stress disorder or a single mother struggling to pay the bills and raise her children alone, we all experience trying times at some point in life. Kinsler's "Think Snow" mentality and mantra helped him survive many battles – both on and off the battlefield. I think you'll find that, when applied to everyday life, this same mentality can work miracles for others as well.

We've all got a story to tell. Our lives are stories – and each day is a new chapter. We can't re-write history, but we can re-record history. We can't predict the future, but we can change our story (or our lives) and essentially effect the outcome of our lives. Everyone has a story. Some are sad, some are happy, some are true, some are embellished, some connect deeply with us and some have no meaning other than to the person who wrote it. Nonetheless, it would be a shame to take our stories to the grave where they are forever lost.

Many will debate the age-old question of whether there is life after death. I say it depends on how you define "life." Can an author pour his wisdom, experiences, and "life" into a book? – And will that book still be around long after the author has departed? The answer is yes; therefore, I conclude that you can live long after you are gone by sharing your life through writing.

It takes courage to share your innermost feelings and sometimes, your deepest, darkest secrets. You'll discover as you read this book, courage is an essential ingredient for survival in a foreign country, halfway around the world, in the midst of a war in which the enemy is not clearly defined.

Time after time, you'll feel the courage that Kinsler and his comrades exhibited as you take a walk in their shoes (or boots) as you cautiously meander through the dense jungle as stories from the front lines of America's most controversial war unravel on the pages of this book. Kinsler, a self-described "grunt," dramatically communicates to me that he and the other grunts were "lions who were led by lambs." I can empathize with him and the plight that the soldiers faced during the war because I believe that this profound statement holds true today – not just in war, but leadership is lacking in many areas of our society today. I see voids of leadership in today's family and their values (or lack thereof). Mediocre parenting coupled with a lack of leadership in our school systems are robbing our youth of a life full of possibility and potential – much like many good men were robbed of their life during the war in Nam. The lack of strong leadership in businesses can stifle growth and squander profitability – even the brightest minds and greatest personalities cannot shine in a non-conducive environment with negative leadership. I won't digress into my feelings on lack of leadership in politics because Kinsler does a masterful job of covering that topic in the pages of this book.

Kinsler's story is particularly interesting to me because my father was also in Vietnam during the same time period. I've tried on many, many occasions to persuade my father into telling me about his experiences in the war – and on each occasion, he curtly responds that "he doesn't want to talk about it and will never talk about it." My father has never given me any indication that he suffers from any kind of post-traumatic war syndrome; he just chooses not to replay the events - and I respect that.

There were, however, a couple of instances when my father "accidentally" released a few thoughts about Vietnam while in my presence. I must have been around thirteen years old in one case. We were driving around town and my father was checking on some properties (he was a Realtor at the time). I was probably nagging him about being hungry in a bratty, spoiled, know-it-all, teenage kind of attitude. My father listened to me whine about as long as he could stand it. When we pulled up to a stoplight, he turned to me with one of the sternest faces I'd ever seen him wear and he said only two words "sixteen days." He then turned his attention back to the red light in front of us. I persisted and demanded to know what the heck "sixteen days" had to do with my growling stomach. To which he replied, "Try going sixteen days with no food. Watch your friend eat a rat. Then tell me how fucking hungry you are." Not only did he not say another word for the rest of the ride, but he also had never previously cursed in my presence. I quickly shut my mouth - and lost my appetite.

I felt a strong sense of appreciation for what my father must have endured and I felt a strong sense of gratitude for the fact that I had never experienced such deprivation or suffering in my life. I think most Patriotic Americans can appreciate the suffering and sacrifice that many brave military men and women give so that we can enjoy freedom and life in the greatest nation this world has ever known. When one thinks of a soldier's sacrifice and suffering the following may come to mind: Time away from loved ones and even losing impatient loved ones in the process. Missing out on watching children grow up. Holidays away from home. Physical injury and death would be the obvious choice for many when asked what a soldier's maximum sacrifice could be.

But what if those who fought and died for our country were the "lucky ones?" And what if those who lived on after the war to lament over those who were lost or missing - and who "lost" themselves and their former life and way of thinking and viewing the world were the true casualties of the war? Post-traumatic stress disorder (PTSD) plagues many of our country's greatest heroes.

Depression, anxiety, fear, lack of self-confidence and laziness plague millions of Americans who have never seen a uniform – let alone a battlefield. In my estimation, I expect that many people will realize that they've never truly had a "bad day" until they read this book and walk a mile in a grunt's boots.

If you are experiencing a bad day or a string of bad luck, "Think Snow" and keep on marching on!

God works in mysterious ways and sometimes help comes in interesting packages. Kinsler survived the war, but the battle within him continued for over four decades until he finally met his match – an eight year old little girl. The rest is "his story." Enjoy the journey.

Chapter 1
Lost in Space

It was as if some alien force had scooped me right up out of my own life and dropped me off on a foreign planet. To say that my situation was out of control would be a statement of epic disproportion. My emotions were running wild. Whatever I had done up to this point in time - good or bad, right or wrong, came to an end; a definitive finish. The world just stopped.

When you're lost, at least you know you came from somewhere, but I did not even have a point of reference. I wished for one of those maps outside the restroom on I-95 with an indicator pointing to a little spot with the message saying "You Are Here."

I was empty - drained of energy, novocained from the neck up, without a clue of what was guiding my life or carrying me on this horse with no name. Or was I dreaming?

The smell of the C-4 that was heating my coffee brought me down to reality a bit. Strangely, I thought that someday I would be rewarded for going through this - or something to that effect. I could not sort out my thoughts, so I listened instead. Listening was the only thing that made sense, but the vanilla cookies in my C-rations tasted super after being dunked in the hot coffee, so I had another one.

It's hard to recapture moments you have purposely forgotten for 40 years, but no matter how much I tried to erase them, they remained. They're always there and they've always been there. They never go away. They just never leave. I felt like I was body surfing huge waves at the beach (which is great fun), but you surrender all control.

It was a moment like no other- then I realized that something even more unusual was happening to me. My normal routine ended abruptly. Something shifted into overdrive. I could feel it, sense it, and experience it, but I still had no control. It was as if I was a caged animal at the zoo and all of my buddies were outside peering in with their mouths wide open in disbelief.

Suddenly, I heard Hueys. Were they coming down to pick us up - or were they dropping off more grunts?

I was confused – so confused that I wasn't sure if it was my own bewilderment or if it was my buddies who were confused.

Have you ever had a piece of spinach stuck prominently between your front teeth? Everyone knows it's there – except you. Some people just stare at the spinach and others totally ignore its existence.

I tried my best to be present to that moment, but the waves of irrational thought were pounding me like the helpless body surfer who is about to face plant into a sand bar. My thoughts were so loud I could have sworn my buddies were hearing them as I walked - or should I say, hovered, without my feet touching the red slippery ground.

As I drank my coffee, the smell of burning wood and the unmistakable and ever present stench of rotten human flesh filled my nose. Nauseated, I tried to shake it off my thoughts and my connection to all external senses.

Today, our platoon was to be rewarded for a job well done. Ha! Imagine that. Two weeks earlier we spent three days climbing to the top of a mountain in Quan Duc Province. Less than half of us walked back down on our own steam.

My nerves were tweaking as a result of the internal galvanizing that was coming to me and through me after this intense firefight. I looked like someone had touched me with defibrillator paddles, but it wasn't someone – it was something, some hideous thing no human being should ever do to another human being.

The horror of Nam was sinking in early and I could sense my mind beginning to shut down.

The chow showed up at 2:00 in the afternoon, just in time for a monsoon rain to fuck everything up.

My moment of surrealism; however, remained intact.

The salt in my sweat had starched my shirt and pants with the most interesting white waves of design radiating in all directions – some looking like a chart of the Dow Jones or Nasdaq results for the day just before the hammer comes down at 4 o'clock (which was the least of my actual concerns), but for some strange reason caught my attention. I couldn't stop studying my body's creativity, but then I couldn't stop anything - so it seemed ok to just stare at the waves in my shirt as long as I wanted to.

This twilight zone appeared to have no end in sight.

I wanted to wake up - or go to sleep. I cannot recall which. Reality was elusive, so there was no other recourse except to just move into another day without a clue of what was happening - with or without thinking.

Then there was this rush kinda' thing that became addictive. I would discover much later that when it takes over, it entices you to live on a tightrope. It becomes a high you look forward to - like a happy hour at your favorite watering hole back home after a long hard day's work.

I only knew that the wave was taking me wherever it wanted to, yet there was this awareness of change that wasn't subject to the calendar's demand of recognition.

One can travel east endlessly without ever going west, but I was going north - and north was changing into due south! My internal compass succumbed to the vertigo from the spinning rotor blades of the Hueys and the rifling lines inside the barrel of my M-16. Cause and effect was setting in and taking over. There was nothing to manage anymore. We were expressionless pawns being sacrificed without reason on a board void of squares.

The day after Christmas, I choppered out to my first assignment in the field. The recognition or celebrating of holidays disappeared into a year without months as well as months without weeks and weeks without days. I was a replacement, so I traveled alone.

Some branches of the military utilize the buddy system — meaning that you serve in active duty with the guys you trained with for many months prior to your tour of duty. This creates a spirit of camaraderie as you grapple with all of the radical changes surrounding you in your transition from civilian life to that of the military. But in the Army, in the 60's, you were made to feel like a number – or just a piece of meat hanging on a conveyer - waiting to be processed - systematically and forcibly moving toward a date in time when your number, printed on a tag, tied to a string, will dangle from your big toe.

As a replacement, you're always alone - and you have to deal with it. You have no friends, no buddies. You are a number - nothing more!

In the late 60's, the killed, wounded, and missing in action numbered in the hundreds every day - creating a huge demand for replacements. Fortunately for me, I was aware of the conveyer belt and its demanding pull – even at the ripe old age of 26. But that did not erase my sadness as I watched the procession of little lost puppies walking down the middle of the street in the cold rain - shivering and shaking from the fears of being lost, abandoned and alone. I was surrounded by dead and dying young men.

There was no time to make friends in the boonies! I found out rather quickly that it was not a good idea to get too close to anyone. Guys were getting zapped before you could remember their names, so most of us used nick names. It was much easier to put them in bags if you didn't know their names.

I was the only grunt on the chopper. As usual, I rode alone - along with some ammo and water. Upon landing, no words were exchanged – a sergeant simply pointed to the center of the company perimeter and said "Go see the old man."

The old man turned out to be the captain of the first company I was assigned to as a grunt. He was greatly respected as a leader while maintaining a stand-offish façade to anyone under his rank.

I headed in that direction, but some guys called me over to their platoon bunker – they needed the replacement and they knew it was me. It was my first warm greeting in many months. We chatted - telling each other where we were from in the states (which as I was to find out was THE most important piece of info needed about everyone there).

It was getting dark, so they told me to get my ammo and report to Captain H. He took my paperwork and told me to grab some M-16 ammo and grenades.

I was bewildered as I stared at a small mountain of ammunition, so I asked him "How many should I take?"

He grinned sarcastically, yet seriously as he answered "As much as you can carry without passing out."

The ARC lights started as soon as night set in. The Air Force B-52's laid a path of death two miles wide and one hundred miles long practically every night. Each bomber would cover a twenty mile stretch - which called for five sorties to accomplish the mission. Each ARC, or bomb laced itself into the next and looked like the bottom of Grandma's tablecloth in the dining room - only upside down. The western sky was rumbling and the puffs of light went from south to north. They put me to sleep like a baby being rocked in his momma's arms who was getting accustomed to life outside of the safety of her womb. The paradigm shift of welcoming the sounds of bombs putting me to sleep rather than the thoughts of what was happening to the enemy as they hit the earth eased into my mind without notice.

I was the oldest guy in the company, except for my First Sergeant, so I became known as "GRAMPS" (which did not bother me for some reason). The stigmas that were normally coupled to age remained back home. There, age mattered to your would-be employer - or the girl sitting at the bar, born twenty years before you, who was giving you the "inviting eye" and the confidence you needed to approach her. Here, how much longer you were going to live was the background music that played every day, all day – as it does in the heartbeat of warriors in all wars.

Time waits for no man, but it becomes a more than precious commodity when you erase the future of a man in the sights of your M-16.

Our routine dictated that we did not stay in any one place very long – this remained very consistent.

We would hump the boonies for a few days, set up on top of a mountain in a circle, run patrols and night ambushes, conduct daily sweeps around our perimeter about one thousand feet out, and set up listening posts each night (which consisted of three man teams which would set up 100 feet outside the perimeter with a radio in order to be an early warning to the company of nearby movement). We also executed search and kill or search and destroy missions in a never-ending need to find the enemies' store houses of ammo and guns. We also conducted LRRP's (long ranged recon patrols); which were seven man teams sent out several klicks away from firebases for five or six days to lay low and observe enemy movement of any type. LRRP's were not to engage Charlie unless absolutely necessary. Only seasoned grunts went on LRRP's.

Most of the time, in fact, the majority of our time, was spent humping mountains - up and down, in and out, through ridge lines and valleys, sideways and zigzags.

We sounded like pigs grunting and groaning - ergo the handle "GRUNTS". We even looked like pigs covered with mud. We ate like pigs - and we smelled like pigs. Most of the time, we felt like pigs too.

My large green bath towel was my best friend. I never knew I could sweat that much. You learn quickly how to survive by not wearing socks or underwear - along with the hundreds of other tricks needed to survive. One of the strangest changes in my anatomy was typical of the instinctual survival mechanisms placed in us all. I hardly ever peed. My body was holding on to all the water it needed for life. The toxins were coming out of the largest gland in our bodies; our skin. In spite of all the stress of daily life, I slept like a baby. I could sleep soaking wet in the rain while being bit by God only knows what - and at times through a mortar bombardment without waking up, because my body desperately needed sleep.

The elements in Vietnam were tougher than the enemy, but not tougher than our bodies!

I told myself over and over that I was not going to die in this God forsaken armpit of the world, but a part of me was not listening or not totally convinced.

My friends said I was not the "Ken" they knew when I came back home. Oh Well!

V told us he was going home on a five day leave to marry his pregnant girlfriend. He had only been in country three weeks when he got the letter from her. All of the arrangements had been made for his flight home the next day.

His girlfriend's time to deliver their baby was set in stone and so was V's fate.

"Time is the King of men; He is both their parents, and he is their grave, and gives them what he will, not what they crave." – Shakespeare

V was a quiet, easy going guy who did not say a whole lot about anything. He kept to himself - which was okay with all the other grunts in our platoon.

The 17th day of January 1968 was a pivotal day. It was an Alice in Wonderland kind of day – full of adventure down into the rabbit hole. It was a first day at school. It was like the first time you drive dad's car all by yourself. It was a day of reckoning. There was a dictum coming up from within me that I did not want to hear or respond to with regret, so I treated it like a report card full of C's and D's that I had to take home to Mom and Dad. It had to start, it had to happen. It was why I was there - and I knew that, but I was so scared I felt like my blood was coming out of the pores of my skin on that day.

My squad was going on a sweep that morning, which would take us well into the late afternoon to complete.

As soon as we got outside our company perimeter, we could smell the snuffed out cooking fires in the heavy air of the morning. The torrential daily rains turned the ground into mush and forced it to hold onto all its' foul odors - like those that emanate from a dirty sponge in the kitchen sink that should have been discarded weeks prior.

That was the day of the big shift. It was a moment locked in time like the afternoon when you finally decide to straighten out your top dresser drawer and you see that old weather beaten Timex you meant to get a new battery for 25 years ago - still telling you it's 2:32. It was a stop and a start. It was the wave that came from behind and carried me and pushed me and left me alone on an unfamiliar shore.

We were on the side of a ridgeline when we spotted two V.C. (Viet Cong) cooking some rice down in a valley about 400 feet away. After a short whispered discussion, it was decided the M-79 could handle the job. But they slipped into the thick bush as soon as they heard the "pop pop" of the gun, so we kept walking after calling in to report how we fucked up what should have been two easy kills. We were all greener than green.

It turned out that the V.C. outnumbered the mosquitoes that day - which was noticed by all of us, but not discussed verbally - evidenced only with non-verbal communications.

The coolness of the morning departed as the steam sprouted up - ushering in the stillness of the sweltering heat of a mid-day sauna bath. The jungle reeked with the remnant odors of fish heads and rice, along with burnt charcoal, black feces and piss from the V.C.

Two of our guys had the runs, which caused us to stop every 20 minutes. We took a break to eat around 12:00. Three LP's (listening posts) were deployed.

V was one of the three. I had not yet opened my first can of c-rations when the AK-47's opened up and confirmed our unspoken fears of this day. It was over before it started as two of the L.P's returned. I was sent to see about the third.

I crept on my hands and knees out to where V was positioned. He was sitting with his back resting on a tree, but I could only see his stationary right arm.

The silence screamed with echoes of spent ammo and hot brass was everywhere. I was on my belly using my elbows and knees to support myself - just like when I fixed a leaky cold water pipe underneath our house back home. As I inched my way to V, I remembered how much I hated doing that plumbing job - and this was no different. January 17, 1968 was one of those days for me. By "one of those days", I mean one of those days that tries a man's soul. One of those days that we must creep into to fix the brokenness.

I called V's name as I crept closer. His arm still didn't move. I reached around the tree to pull him down but my hand went into his chest. There was no telling how many rounds he took. Charlie caught him "eating" or "half-steppin" as was the term we used when someone got zapped.

We never talked about what happened on that day. "Don't mean nothin" became our catch phrase - which was applied to everything your mind would try to explain or rationalize. Each new day had all of our attention. Twenty four hours became a lifetime to hang onto and live to the fullest. Tomorrow would begin again - back in the world at the end of 365 lifetimes. Where we were was not part of the world you see! Even its beauty, the beauty of the mountains was invisible – besides, there was no time to look.

It was like waking up in the recovery room after your colonoscopy and thinking, "When are they going to do the procedure?" And then you realize, "You mean it's over? I can go home now?"

Forty years later my psychologist told me "You're okay. It's over, Ken. You can enjoy your life. That was then - and now is now. You can go home now."

We put V in a body bag and called for a dust off. His name and what happened on that day was never mentioned again.

The old man called for us to return to the company perimeter. It was getting close to the hottest part of the day when we started heading back. The genesis to kill was calling for more from all of us after that day - and that beginning would have no end.

My towel was now soaked in sweat which actually kept me cool as it reversed its purpose. What I didn't realize was that the perspiration was ridding me of the fears of my first firefight in Vietnam. For the first time since my arrival in this country, I was not alone. It was the first for two other guys as well - one of which threw up when he saw all the blood on me from dragging V back - and of course, the gruesome sight of his open chest.

Another first for us was getting accustomed to the blood in between our fingers as it dried. It felt like glue as it held the fingers together. The rainy season would take care of this dilemma, but in the dry season all water was for drinking, so you waited for the blood to dry up, turn black, and then you could pick it off or just forget about it.

An argument erupted about the correct directions to get back to our company. The verbal fight ended when the 2nd Lieutenant made his decision to return in a direction which I doubted, but I kept my mouth shut. We had plenty of time before nightfall - or so we thought. We were only one and a half klicks from the company's location (a klick = 1,000 meters). It seemed like we just started the hump when the AK's opened up again. We walked into an ambush. It was clearly going to be a long day. The Lt. took a round in the leg, our Sergeant E-7 caught one in the arm, and our point man was dead. We called for another dust-off (a med-a-vac Huey which picked up a wounded or dead grunt) after we cut a LZ (landing zone) in the dense jungle. It took forever for the chopper to come, but the flies came right away - along with new fears and new smells of vomit and diarrhea. Charlie started to holler at us because he knew who was in control. We answered his calls by spraying the jungle with our M-16s along with informing them that they were "slant eyed mother fuckers," etc...

All of our leaders were gone - leaving us with an E-5 in charge who did not know how to read a compass - and he

13

had just gotten in country. He didn't have a clue how to get us back to our company and the sun was going down quicker than a Hanoi hooker. I spotted a cluster of unusually tall trees which were in close proximity to our company's location. I remembered them from before, so I told the Sergeant as I pointed out the trees. He decided that we were going to follow my instincts and we moved out in the direction of the trees - with me in the lead. The afternoon rains began as we headed out. It was a welcome rain as it began to wash off the blood from our hands and our clothes, but not off or out of our minds.

"Don't mean nothin."

I began to see why the yesterdays were never brought up.

That dreadful afternoon, I walked through a doorway which led to a room with no exits. Little did I know, none of my tomorrows would ever be the same.

I made a decision that day about my vision, a simple decision - a decision I would not change. My decision was to kill anything that moved. I recall working myself into that state of mind - which I determined was necessary to survive as a grunt. Whatever moved anywhere in my vision – died. It was very simple!

That state of mind was blind to everything except survival. Even all the noble thoughts of duty, honor and country had no resting place in that mind - only survival! Respect for authority had no place in that mind. If anything became a threat to survival and was in vision, it died. It was all about survival from then on.

That day, I led my squad back to our company before sunset without incident or another clash with Charlie. My aforementioned room was meant to be an allegory of a jungle with no way out, so getting back did not mean getting out.

Losing, failing, making mistakes and dying are part of living. The worst thing that can happen at the race track is for you to win a bunch of money the first time you go. There was going to be a great deal of losing, dying and failing in the year ahead of me - and coming out on top of your first go-round can put you in the wrong frame of mind. I am told they teach officers how to fail at West Point. The object being to learn how to fail in the classroom so you can survive on the battlefield, but those instructions should have been given to the grunts as well. Even though we got shot up that day, most of us returned to the company perimeter - so it was considered a win of sorts.

Our minds often find themselves experiencing life without preparation time, so our coping mechanisms kick in automatically like you're on cruise control. It's really a very simple concept, but I didn't know it then and no one even tried to get us prepared. To the contrary, we were the only brainwashed soldiers in the history of the USA. The Vietnamese were de-humanized during our training and in our eyes. We were throwing out the thrash. We were policing up a French mess. This wasn't a war. After all, it only lasted one year.

We fought gooks and dinks, not people - because they didn't even live in the real world!

One afternoon we played soccer with the head of an NVA (North Vietnamese Army) officer. The only thing that mattered was survival. Hey, he was just a gook - we were the people!

We were told that the first 45 days and the last 45 days were when you were most likely to get hit. At first you are "green," and at the end you get over confident. It made perfect sense and proved to be true - time and time again.

We got a new 2nd Lt. who had ambitions of a career in the army with an assignment at the Pentagon to end up his 20 year hitch. The problem was that he was getting in the way of survival. He insisted on being called "Sir" and rejected advice from our new E-7 who had two tours under his belt. I felt sorry for him in a strange way. He wore his fear for all of us to see and it was obvious he had no business being an officer, but sorry Lt's were not the Army's problem - they were the grunts' problem.

We were sent into a city to do some street fighting (which was totally new to us). Up to that point we had only seen jungles. We did better in the cities because we had tanks, artillery, and gunships if needed.

Charlie was retreating quickly and moral was high. My platoon, headed by our green 2nd Lt. was receiving machine gun fire from a building in front of us. There was an open field between us and the building. We had the cover of a tall, stone wall and every time we tried to advance, Charlie's machine gun would rain bullets at our feet - sending us back to the tall, stone wall for cover. We had a flame thrower sent up and I was ordered by the Lt. to run across the field and torch the building while three other guys provided cover fire for me. All of us suggested calling for a gunship to blast the whole building, but the Lt. wanted a decoration for his gallant efforts. I refused to carry the flame thrower to what would be a certain death - and so did all my buddies. The Lt. ranted at us, sounding like a narcissistic nine year old brat screaming at his mother in an amusement park.

What happened then would be repeated throughout the year. The Lt. threatened us all with dis-honorable discharges. He was promptly told by all of us that if he filed the paperwork, he would not wake up the next morning. He knew we meant it, so he asked politely for the radio.

A gunship was called in to drop the building and everyone survived that day.

Someone once said "War is hell." It's more complicated than that - and it isn't what Hollywood makes it out to be either.

Closing doors and walking away cannot make thoughts disappear. The pictures remain and the denials only add to the fires that burn down deep inside us. There are things in life that can only be known through experience and war is one of them.

Second Lt.'s had a very short life span in Nam - as our golden boy was about to find out. My relationship with this particular Lt. became one of those fires that would not go out for decades. Officers had to earn respect in Nam. Honoring authority was bestowed only to those who could gain it through experience and trust.

The momentum was picking up rapidly. We were getting no down time. It was one CA (combat assault) after another. I knew I wouldn't be able to keep up a pace like this for a year - and I wasn't alone. The "lucky ones" among us got a ticket home via a most unpleasant condition known as jungle rot - which is a fungus that eats the skin on your feet, scalp, crotch, or wherever. Some guys got stomach disorders. All of us got insect bites – some of which led to malaria.

Others went to extreme measures to get the hell out of Nam. I watched a guy shoot himself in the foot during a short firefight to punch his ticket home. Another guy ate only peanut butter which caused him severe constipation and a huge case of hemorrhoids; however, it was much less of a pain in the ass than his tour in Nam. He wasn't sent home, just to the rear of the line because he wasn't able to eat c-rations.

Our 2nd Lt. was still with us when we got orders to take a hill near DAK-TO with a company element.

Charlie was dug in well and prepared to fight. This was not what we were accustomed to. It was usually hit and run for us - with the whole firefight lasting just a couple of minutes.

Gunships were called in to help on this hill - and that's when the Lt. lost it. He mistakenly called the mini guns on a huey in on us. He got confused while talking to the chopper pilot about which side of the hill we were located. Fortunately, there were huge trees everywhere which served as cover for us when the choppers made their passes from north to south. Of course Charlie took advantage of the situation and we suffered heavy losses that afternoon and we never got to the top of the hill.

Everyone knew what was about to take place after that. It didn't have to be discussed. A melding of the minds occurred among us to delete our Lt. The days became effortless moves on a chess board for all of us to experience and observe; excluding the Lt. who we kept in check and oblivious to it all. It was amazing for us to watch him go through a day without a clue as to anything being wrong.

Our conversations with the Lt. changed and were tempered with a kind of pity or sadness, rather like watching a helpless animal being sucked into quicksand. His fate was set - it was simply a matter of how and when. The usual talk ended and transitioned into acting out the day instead of living in it. We were putting on a little play for him, but he refused to watch. We were in awe of his blindness to it all. It didn't matter though, we just shook our heads and grinned at each other as we recited our lines in anticipation of the last act as we took control of his fate.

The absence of green in the scenery was accepted without a thought as to why or where it went. We were dropped off on just another mountain which had been dusted with Agent Orange. The idea was for us to get a break and calm down for a few days. Our mountain had also received a few 500 pound bombs in order to insure we wouldn't have any surprise visitors for a little while. They dropped off some hot chow and mail and a bunch of beer. The defoliate had killed off all the bugs and animal life as well as the birds, thus silencing the very nature of the land (which before our arrival was a beautiful, lush, green creation fashioned by centuries of untouched time).

For a moment or two, we began to appreciate the beauty of the mountains and the thick vegetation which surrounded us in all directions. The night sky was cloudless and the moon was so bright you could read letters from home.

We laughed and wondered if they spiked the beer on us as we all opened up and talked about our lives back home. For once, we interacted and communicated like real people who actually cared about things. Usually, the only time reserved for caring was when someone got wounded - and then only briefly because it meant a ticket back to the world for them. When someone got killed it didn't mean anything. The concept of death lost all its meaning. Dying wasn't even called death - grunts got zapped. The sight and smell of dead flesh became a common part of everyday life. In the real world, time was allotted for grief and mourning, but here was not the time or place for that, so grief and mourning lost their meaning. We were more like dogs that sniffed the dead carcass of a fallen friend and then walked away with a blank stare in our eyes.

We savored our little time in limbo to the fullest, knowing full well what the future would hold for us after dispensing with our infamous Lt.

The secrecy of our plan for the Lt. was vital. Everyone knew this kind of stuff happened, and officers tried not to show their fear. Our plan involved acting without a script. The non-verbal communication intensified and the amount of people in the know were always kept to a bare minimum. This was a dangerous game and we wondered how much of it had been played out in other wars.

Our company was assigned a scout dog (German Sheppard) for a couple of weeks because of the kind of mission we were about to be given. All of us were briefed on the dos and don'ts involved with having a scout dog around. He was a one-man dog, so no petting was allowed. If his master got killed, they would put the dog down too. It was great having him with us - you just had to leave him alone and that was the rule you had to follow.

Traditionally, we were never given much info about what was to be accomplished on our combat assaults by chopper. We turned into robots – incapable of emotion or thought. Without any discussion, we would simply barge our way into another day. So right when you thought you had things figured out, yet another surprise would appear. There was no low hanging fruit in the central highlands of South Vietnam - in that nothing was easy.

Our platoon sergeant called us together for a briefing about a CA we were going to execute the next morning. The NVA had overrun a special forces A-camp, killing everyone on the hill. We were going in to clean up the mess.

We decided this was going to be it for the Lt. The plan was simple. In the madness of a hot L.Z. (landing zone), the dog would get confused and attack the Lt. The master of the dog agreed, so the plan was set. It worked like a Swiss watch. Our Lt. got a chewed up knee and a ticket home.

It turned out to be a win-win situation for everyone. We got the best 2nd Lt. in Nam to replace him and the limping Lt. got to go home and brag about what a great hero he was. He was one of the lucky ones. Most of the time, Lt.'s were hit with friendly fire or a frag (hand grenade) was rolled into their hooch in the middle of the night while they slept – they would send the pieces home in a bag. Wow, I've gotten way ahead of myself. In retrospect, it's easy to see how we often get caught up in worlds we didn't choose or design - even as civilians. Nam ironically was like home – only to the "Nth degree".

Chapter 2
Don't Mean Nothin'

So my Big Ben wind up alarm clock went off twenty minutes too soon, as it always did when waking me for work, but this day would be different, very different. This would be the first day of a total loss of controlled life. We took that "one step forward" and swore to support and defend the constitution of the United States against all enemies foreign and domestic as we entered 730 days of surreal existence. The clock started it and the clock would end it, but nothing would stop it – kind of like The Hotel California where you can check out, but never leave.

The bizarre thing is that we're caught up in these worlds that are fashioned by the times we live in, or wake up to, but we need not be molded by them. We always have the power to choose. The miasma of Nam was not able to usurp my power of choice. Thank God!

A good job, a good mate, and dreams of financial security all become carrots dangling in front of the nose of the horses we become in life. Heaven forbid we opt not to follow the carrot, knowing that if we do, we'll stray from the herd and become an odd ball. Hopefully, we isolate ourselves from the herd and cultivate the healthy inner strengths we need to feel good about ourselves. My dad used to tell me, "Don't be one of the boys - be one of the men." My dad was right about a lot of things. At the core of our individual being we were not made to fit in, but to stand out and be unique and different one-of-a-kind creatures who believe in themselves.

Learning without being taught was the key to survival in Vietnam - and this still holds true for me today. Actually, instincts, intuition and deep self-awareness became the only realities. It's ironic how some things just never change.

I was born and raised in one of the biggest industrial cities in America and now that is all over. I was a momma's boy, spoiled for sure, as most of us only children are.

All that was over now, along with a God I thought I knew. No! Now it was a bologna sandwich on white bread with a packet of mustard, three cookies and an apple in a brown bag. Now it was a bus ride from the post office, where I took the oath, to the Buffalo airport and then off to Fort Dix, NJ for four days of orientation and then off to Fort Campbell, KY for eight weeks of boot camp, then to Fort Polk, LA for nine weeks of advanced infantry training, then two weeks of Armored Personal Carrier Driver Training School at Fort Knox, Ky. Now it was time to say good bye to your world, your ex-wife, your son, your mom and dad, your girlfriends, your job, your identity and your dignity. Now it was "kill them fuckin' dinks, man!"

I put the future out of my thinking and lived only in the present moment of the day that I woke up to. Anything that threatened that day could be handled with an M-16 (which made life quite simple and easy to manage actually). There were no consequences - just existence for "one" day. Nothing else mattered - not even the rain could daunt it.

It seems as though song writers and movies allow us to see ourselves in ways we fear to unveil to the worlds we live in. So freedom of expression is snuffed out or suppressed and real living is limited to the lyrics in a tune we sing to ourselves over and over, or a line in a movie that exposes what's actually going on inside us.

Capturing and owning a moment in time, then rehearsing it when I needed to overcome a new and unexpected event became an exercise to be repeated in my new life - even if the moments were beyond description and the new events were as foreign as a city I'd never visited. What we yield to does not conquer us - it liberates us from what we suppress ourselves with, so I was to find out.

I would have never known what was in me if I had not gone to Vietnam.

My internalized core values were to be tested and tried on the opposite side of the globe. The security of being surrounded by loving, caring, compassionate people came to an abrupt and total end. This security was replaced by an environment which was foreign, hostile and unknown - a world beyond description.

So the antithesis of normal acceptable behavior became the norm. Nothing about anything really mattered anymore. In a life without consequences, there are no rules, no laws, and no respect. "Don't mean nothin'" became the response for everything and it fit perfectly for every event - good or bad.

I watched as young men, barely out from under the wings of Mom and Dad, were pushed off of helicopters and into worlds of pain, agony, death, hatred and fear. Young men who hadn't had the time or opportunity to find out who they were found themselves surrounded by other boys - dying while acting out roles not of their choosing.

Factory workers, mailmen, college students, construction workers, artists and businessmen all gathered together to kill people. Screaming for Mommy or calling out to God when injured or during an excessively long firefight became a normal occurrence, but was never discussed afterwards. Not knowing your own breaking point was the greatest of all fears, but then "don't mean nothin'" always fit the bill for the right thing to say after every firefight.

There was so much to learn so quickly. The stakes were high (your life) and your window of opportunity to take it all in was shorter than the span of time you get on a $5 one armed bandit in Las Vegas.

You had to rush and take your time. We had to be quick to respond and slow to observe. "Hurry up and wait" became a popular phrase.

There was a need to depend on each other which was coupled with the desire to be left alone.

The slightest nuance in conversation could trigger a major shift in the direction of how a situation was to be handled without the benefit of time to muse. An hour could be a flash of time that lasted for days in your mind, but never on your lips.

Time ceased to be monitored by our watches - or cared about in terms of days, weeks, or months. The future seemed to disappear - leaving us to talk about nothing other than the day we lived in. Conversations could be about those unbelievably great jelly doughnuts in that German bakery back home - or something like that in the past, but never, never the future. Tomorrows were not discussed in any dimension for any reason. Time existed only in the NOW.

Some days were devoted to cleaning your M-16. Nothing else was talked about. Nothing else mattered. Nothing else was allowed through the gates of that day from sun-up to sun-down. If anyone dared to interject a word not pertaining to an M-16 he would be jeered at like a Rhodes Scholar walking into a biker bar full of Hell's Angels.

The only welcome interruption to any day in Vietnam was mail call - and even that would be dreaded by some in anticipation of a "Dear John'" letter.

My Dad would send me sticks of pepperoni, hot sauce, cheese and other treats. He would also strategically hide a pocket size bottle of good whiskey right in the center of my box of goodies. I was everybody's friend when the mail came in. One time my Dad just sent me a letter with no box of treats. I was thrown out of my hooch into the rain and told to instruct my Dad to never mail me another word without some whiskey to accompany it. I did and he never messed up again. Somehow we maintained the uncanny ability to laugh at everything.

At home, we eat together, go to church together, go to the movies together, and go to bars and baseball games together. In Nam, we killed together. We would argue about who zapped this guy or that guy. We shot dead gooks for laughs, live gooks for survival, and suspicious gooks just in case. We shot into the bush without seeing gooks. We shot up into thick trees hoping a gook would fall out. When there were no gooks, we shot hogs and dogs, water buffalo and elephants. We came to shoot - and that is what we did. As Grunts, we learned how to shoot first, but not talk later.

When on police calls, as buck privates back in basic training in Fort Campbell, KY, we would hear the following as we would get in line and walk across the grounds around the mess hall as we picked up cigarette butts and trash: "Pick up everything that doesn't move, if it moves shoot it, if you can't pick it up, paint it!" It was a silly, but true phrase known by everyone who was in the Army. Little did we know the drill instructors were preparing us for our future: when you are in the Army, you shoot!

If your M.O.S. (military occupational specialty) was 11 Bravo (infantry offensive and defensive combat operations), you entered into a passionate relationship with your weapon. You eat with it at your side, you lay it on your knees when you shit, you sleep with it next to you like it's your lover, and you protect it like it's your treasure. You clean it before you clean your body and you share it as much as you share your wife.

We wanted to go into a town once, but we had to turn our weapons in at the guard station in order to not offend the local citizenry. There were restaurants and shops and it looked like a great way to spend an afternoon. I argued with the M.P.'s about the protocol. In the end, we decided not to go.

We all walked away saying "We didn't come to Vietnam to have lunch and shop - or fuck their women, but rather to shoot people."

After all, it wasn't supposed to be an enjoyable afternoon, so why pretend.

It was amazing how the lush, peaceful landscape could transition into a field of fear and anger without warning. How an innocent campfire could erase all previous memories of what they used to be in an instant was a mystery. The good memories were fading into an abyss of an irretrievable bottomless past.

On rare occasions, one of us would vent. All eyes glanced at each other and then bounced over to the guy who opened himself up. This was a sign that he was getting close to losing it. So for a brief moment, we got in touch with our feelings and would throw him a rope with a few laughs or a kind gesture. Others would pay no attention whatsoever to what was happening as your gold fish would do in the living room aquarium while you stare at them.

It took all day to get to the top of the hill "whatever." We suffered a lot of losses. Dust offs were coming in constantly. We finally had to fade back and have the planes take over. The sun was going down and for some unknown reason the hill had to be taken that day. How anyone could survive 500 pound bombs and napalm, I don't know! But when we assaulted hill "whatever" for the final time we were getting shot up again. This time, however, we went to the top and ended the fight with M-16's and machine guns.

The smells melted into each other - the strongest being that of ruptured intestines. The smoke acted like a mixing spoon, blending the foul odors that seemed to be chained to the ground due to the lack of even the slightest breeze. We were told to dig in, which meant Charlie was going to hit us that night. It was the dry season, so the rain, which normally washed up our messes, was not coming. We had to act quickly.

A young NVA soldier, who had been hit, was still warm on top of the hill. He was trying to dig some shrapnel or a bullet out of his stomach with two sticks of bamboo. His hands were still holding the sticks when he died from several rounds of our small arms fire in our final assault to the top. His eyes were open and a calm, peaceful expression was on his face. I thought how strange it was to see him like that. I felt like I knew him – or maybe was his friend in another life. I decided to use his hole in the ground for the night. There was just enough time to fill some sandbags and put out our claymores before nightfall.

The moon was as bright as the sun that night. I went through my friend's sack and found pictures of his wife, kids and letters from home. I was dog tired but I decided to bury him that night, right next to me. The ground was soft from the bombs loosening up the soil, so it didn't take long and it felt like the right thing to do for a friend that I had just killed.

Chapter 3
A Voice in the Wilderness

It was actually cold the next morning. I knew the sun would chase away the chill, and along with it, the memory of a cool Buffalo, NY daybreak and drive to work.

I couldn't remember if I had cleaned my M-16, but then I really didn't care very much right then.

The thought came almost like a voice. I looked over my shoulder to see who was there. I heard it loud and clear, or at least I thought so. "I'm not going to die in this place! I will not die here!"

Over and over with different little variations, I heard the same voice saying "My life is not over! I will not die in this jungle! I am not going to die here!"

I wondered if I had put some of the whiskey my Dad sent me in my morning coffee.

The sound of the chopper blades blew away my mental vacation and suddenly I remembered my M-16 was so dirty I couldn't cock it! I found the oil, squirted it all over, popped in a clip, chambered the first round, pissed on Vietnam and jumped in the chopper. I looked at the grave of my friend and apologized in my mind to his wife and kids.

The boom box on the chopper was screaming "We gotta get out of this place, if it's the last thing we ever do... girl there's a better place for me and you..." I looked down again to where my Viet Cong friend was buried and almost felt human - just for a nano second.

We had just gotten two new guys with their fresh, clean fatigues, shiny new M-16s, and scared shitless looks on their faces. Then I thought, I don't care because I am not going to die today. I do not care about anything let's just get it on!

We were flying north for what seemed like an unusually long time. Something was up and all of us knew it except the NFG's (New Fucking Guys). We were flying high to avoid small arms fire. The ride felt like the ending part of a roller coaster with subtle bumps and flat spots. The door gunners were firing at small groups of NVA which all of us could see. Now and again, they would throw smoke grenades into the larger groups. The planes followed, dropping napalm on the colored smoke - charging the atmosphere with thunder and fire. We turned the volume up on the boom box.

I was sitting on the side of the chopper with my feet on the landing rail. A round came up through the floor, splitting the aluminum diamond plate inches from my butt and then it continued up through the roof of the chopper above me.

The pilot and co-pilot began to scream at each other and the door gunners got into it with each other as well. Our Huey was now leaving a trail of brown smoke behind us and we were losing altitude quickly.

I pulled my camera out to get a few quick shots, but the pictures weren't needed to remember the day ahead of me.

Some days were nothing but a wait, others didn't allow for a thought, still others swept you into a whirlwind of blinding red dust, muzzle flashes, and the sound of bullets cracking as they passed by your head. And of course, the screaming from getting hit with a bullet or a hot piece of shrapnel caused never ending hollering over the radios.

This day would be different from all the others though. This day proved to be a welcomed change. It was like the first day of autumn – in that it could be sensed - like when you open the back door in the morning and take in the cool crisp air for the first time after a long, hot summer, and then light up your first Camel cigarette, and then head off to the garage while wondering if you put enough anti-freeze in the radiator.

Our distressed Huey was heading toward the base of a huge mountain which was being peppered by Charlie's mortar fire. This was not business as usual. I suddenly got a headache - which seemingly came out of nowhere. We crashed and hit the ground hard - far short of our LZ (landing zone). The grass was tall and our rotor blade was cutting through bamboo, but we were all just glad to be on the ground and still in one piece. The silence of the jungle swallowed the sounds of the roaring motors of our chopper as all of its systems gradually slowed down to a stop. The squelch of the radio broke the dead silence and then the familiar crack of the AK-47's took over.

Two other choppers dropped off about 20 grunts close to us for support. When Charlie saw he was outnumbered, he disappeared after a short firefight. We waited for a Chinook to haul our crippled Huey away and then we humped off to the base of the mountain not far off in the distance.

We took a break in what used to be a small, but heavily used railway station. I could almost feel the activity of what it used to be decades ago. The rain had washed away most of the railroad tracks and the grass and bamboo now hid the roads leading into and away from what once was a bee hive of activity. Corrugated sheet metal and flat sheets of tin now covered the windows and doors of little shops and restaurants that surrounded the terminal building with its ramps and stairs at both ends. I wandered off by myself (which is something I had never done), but for some reason I wanted to be alone. I tried to imagine what it would have been like to stop here for a bite to eat 50 years ago as a tourist. I was enjoying my little mental vacation until a rat ran in front of me and then scurried under a door. My return to reality turned into a cold sweat when I realized I had not heard nor seen any of my buddies for what seemed like an eternity.

My imagination was still alive through, as I swore I could hear the sounds of an old steam engine approaching the loading ramp I was standing on. I heard the train whistle blow and watched the steam blowing out of the big smoke stacks as the coal car, and finally the caboose, crept along out of the jungle and stopped alongside the ramp. My momentary daydream was interrupted when I heard the welcome sounds of my buddies' voices coming through the tall grass.

I felt welcomed in that place and wanted to stay (which was more than just a new thought), but rather a new way to think.

I didn't want to kill anyone there, so I left as soon as its grip released me.

Life was turning out to be like owning a car you can drive, but don't know how to fix. Every day took me places I couldn't change or improve, but each new day placed me in the driver's seat behind the wheel again.

Nothing would bring the train station back to life, and knowing that didn't help me accept it as reality, but killing people just didn't seem like the right thing to do there.

My mind returned to the "abnormal normal" back in the bush. I sensed the transition immediately. The train station was a place for living and enjoying life's encounters - like meeting strangers traveling on business or pleasure. The jungle was reserved for bleeding, dying, hatred and killing.

We walked into a large clearing which led to the foot of our mountain destination. I had never seen this much activity outside of a basecamp - ever. Choppers were everywhere - along with jeeps, trucks and APC's (Armored Personnel Carriers). A battery of 105's were being set up. Engineers were stringing wire and the TOC (Tactical Operations Center) was being built in the middle of the chaos.

My platoon Sergeant told me to get a jeep, fill it with empty sandbags and take the NFG's up to the top of the mountain. The access road was peppered with craters from mortars and bombs, but the jeep could handle it, so off we went. Small arms fire was popping and whizzing by us from every direction (which was ignored by everyone except the NFG's). It took a while to adjust to the fact that people were shooting at you and threatening your life. After a while, you become able to discern which threats are far enough away to just get your attention and those which require you to get down and seek cover.

I stopped for a minute, got the names of the NFG's and told them to calm down. They were soaked in sweat and as pale as ghosts, so I started to joke around a bit to try and calm them down. I asked where they were from, briefed them about what had been going on and what we were going to do next.

I remember hearing myself repeat to them what a Sergeant (who turned out to be one of my best friends when I first got in the country) said to me. "Don't think - just do what I tell you!"

So I eyeballed my two new friends and gave 'em the line again – this time real loud, because the gun fire was getting closer and the mortars were starting to pop in the distance. I down shifted our jeep and went into four wheel drive. The tension was mounting, but manageable.

The 105 howitzers were firing for effect behind us from the firebase and the rumble of the jets now flooded the sky - spreading the unmistakable smells of burning woods, expended mortars, and death. The dominant odor was always rotting or burning flesh.

The mountain we were ascending was a hill of great pain - echoing its cries of horror above all other sounds. You could almost feel the pathos of what had happened just hours before we were there. The atmosphere had a weight to it so heavy that normal breathing became laborious.

The notion of what took place there remained and impeded our forward motion - kind of like the old ball and chain used on prisoners centuries ago.

I drove over downed barbed wire, hoping not to get a flat tire, because my primary objective was getting to the top of the mountain. For a brief second, I thought about driving through the lush mountains of Kentucky and Tennessee. I remembered how the clouds would remain in the valleys until the morning sun would dry them up – and then they would rise into the sky of a warm, friendly, new day.

Mountains are beautiful no matter where they are on earth. They're so majestic and noble as they lift us up so we can appreciate the beauty of nature from their heavenly vantage point, but this mountain was fighting the presence of the humans who were pimping its purpose.

We finally made it to the top of the mountain and discovered a well-established A-camp that appeared to have been there for many months.

A-camps were outposts manned by roughly 14 or so Army Special Forces soldiers and 100 or so CIDG's (civilian irregular defense groups) also referred to as a MIKE FORCE. Together, they would establish a very secure defensive perimeter and then run ambushes, re-con patrols and covert missions.

This particular A-camp had been overrun by the NVA. Our planes had eliminated all life on the mountain after the massacre, but the NVA still surrounded the foothills of the camp as they doctored their wounded while a clean-up effort was accomplished before our arrival with the sandbags. All of this had just taken place - as evidenced by the blood soaked terrain everywhere we looked.

The heat of the day hit us like opening the oven door to check on the Thanksgiving Day turkey. My two green buddies looked like senior citizens in a nursing home with their mouths hanging open waiting for dinner to be served.

I broke the silence as I continued driving up, "Remember, do whatever I tell you - don't think! Got it?"

They nodded as I hit the brakes. There was a barren nob of red dirt with a large sandbagged bunker in the middle of it which was surrounded by smaller bunkers. There wasn't a living soul in sight.

From the driver's seat of the jeep, I looked back to where we came from and was shocked to realize how far away we now were from all the activity below us.

My first thought was how unusual it was to not to see anyone up here. My second thought was "oh shit!" as an RTO ran out of his bunker screaming "Incoming!"

We heard the thump, thump, thump! I pointed to two bunkers and screamed at my new buddies "Go!"

The first mortar round hit next to our jeep - flipping it on its side. The second was a dud and the third hit the road behind us.

It was proving to be a most interesting day for sure, and it was still morning!

I dove head first into a hole leading to a bunker and was shocked to see a man who instantly became one of the most unforgettable characters in my life. He was kind of like one of those people you read about in one of those "Readers Digest" articles you pick up while in the dentist office waiting room. He was an old man with deep wrinkles in his face and neck, burnt red skin, long gray hair that probably used to be blue-black in color, and a smile from ear to ear that was warmer than a cozy fire in a ski lodge. He wore no uniform of any kind and had a long knife in a sheath on his hip. He plainly and clearly said, in perfect English "It'll be over soon."

And somehow I knew it would – just because he said it.

I asked him who he was with - and I no more than got the words out of my mouth when I realized it was a question to which I would not get an answer.

The mortars were subsiding and the small arms had stopped, but my strange "comrade in arms" and I decided to stay low and talk. We took advantage of a moment in time which we both knew was there for us to grab. He said he worked alone, mostly in the north. I didn't ask what tribe he belonged to because it didn't matter. He carried no gun, no radio, and no paper - only the knife. He said he liked what he did, but gave no specifics - only that he would go up around Hanoi, look around for a month or so, then go to Thailand, and then back again.

We shook hands, exchanged well wishes and said good bye. His hand felt like a baseball glove, but his eyes had compassion and love in them. He was quick and nimble for his age and he moved like an Olympic gymnast. I thought to myself, "this guy is 65 years old or my name isn't Ken."

Nobody saw him but me, and I wondered if I had actually seen him myself. The whole incident was like waking up after my appendix was already taken out and asking when they were going to do the surgery!

Life's full of in's and out's, but you never know when it's taking place - until it's over. Not knowing evolved into not caring. Not caring turned into not feeling. Not feeling translated into not living. And not living eased us into a "morphined existence" void of meaning - interrupted only briefly and occasionally by a train station or an old Indian. These, however, became the events that would bring a desire to look forward to the tomorrows.

Back home, life was a boring series of Thursdays connected only by six other days of meaningless existence. Life in Vietnam became one continuous adrenalin rush. Having to deal with the fact that you could be eating ham and lima beans one minute, and then put in a plastic bag the next, forced your mind into an unknown gear - moving forward without a destination.

There was a need to deal with reality every day - and when anyone opted to deny what was going on and tried to escape from what we had to contend with, it was noticed immediately and time was marked by those who watched the attempt.

Back home it was okay to understand why things took place last week or last year, but in the jungle, past, present and future existed in every moment of every day - which resulted in a deep appreciation for the otherwise ignored simple acts of kindness from anyone who was willing to risk being transparent.

My company had seen a good deal of fighting in my first six months, so we acquired something of a reputation. Rumor had it that when a VC or NVA soldier produced one of our patches from a dead grunt, they would get some R & R.

Along with our reputation came the dirtiest missions - the worst of which were night ambushes. We only conducted them while in heavy concentrations of the enemy. The objectives were to engage if we thought we could kill them all - or just observe and count when we were outnumbered. It sounds simple enough, but something always went wrong, so we never took green guys (NFG's) on ambushes - unless we had to.

It was the rainy season, which made whatever you did more difficult. We were close to Cambodia, trying to cut off the enemy's supply lines. The B-52's were doing their nightly bombing runs very close to our positions. The ground vibrated and the atmosphere was electrified with waves of power from the bombs every night.

A re-con team was sent out to find a good spot while seven of us got ready for the night. We took an M-60 machine gun, seven L.A.W.S. (long range anti-tank weapon), as many grenades as we could carry, a radio, and several claymore mines.

Preparation was important and communication was vital. Everyone had to know what to do instinctively because no talking was allowed – ever!

During our planning, we would sit and talk for hours about what if this or what if that happens - along with how and when - until madness set in. The slightest fuck-up during a night ambush meant everybody dies - which we all knew, but didn't want to admit or discuss.

The key player was, of course, the Sergeant in charge. We would lie on our bellies 4 feet apart, touching each other only with the heels of our boots. No talking is ever allowed - only eye contact and finger pointing. The radio was off, thus eliminating the threat of noise from breaking squelch announcing an incoming call. No coughing, farting, burping, hiccupping, or swatting mosquitoes. You could not brush your teeth, smoke, move around, or scratch - and if it was cool outside, you breathed into your towel in order to avoid producing a mist with your breath. The machine gun was in the middle of us and a line of claymores were placed 50 feet from our position. A field of fire 30 feet wide, made of pure hell, awaited any VC or NVA who tripped a wire igniting a flare.

Surprise was our best weapon - stupidity or a sneeze was our worst enemy.

Re-con selected a great spot with lots of thick cover for us that overlooked a large clearing below with no cover or trees for Charlie to hide in. It was ideal in every way.

The moon was almost full - giving us plenty of light and time to catch Charlie with his pants down in an open field full of short grass with nowhere to run or hide.

We got into position at sundown as we expected the un-expected in every way possible. We didn't have to wait very long. To the right and left of our open field was thick jungle, so we had a "shooting gallery" in front of us about the size of a football field. It was around 10:00 pm when an NVA trooper eased out of the thick jungle to our right. He walked slowly, heading across the open field in the moonlight toward our left. He was then followed by another, and another, and another - each keeping about twenty feet between each other. None of us moved an eyelash while we waited for our E-5 to take the first shot. He didn't, so the four NVA troopers walked into the jungle on our left without incident. All of us wondered why we didn't shoot.

Another gook emerged from the jungle on our right and then a procession followed him that lasted most of the night. It was a major troop movement of a battalion or more.

That night, we were eaten alive by ants, mosquitoes and whatever, but we all lived to tell about our adventure - thanks to a sergeant who knew his shit. The first four guys were just a forward element, which none of us knew at that time - except him.

We packed up our gear that glorious morning as we scratched our bites and praised our E-5 all the way back to base camp. He ended up with a promotion to E-6 because he saved all our lives that night. He also proved that some battles aren't worth fighting.

It really is funny how little we know about ourselves until we're forcibly placed into arenas of life that are governed by people who have no names. Strangers simply hold too much sway into our reactions or responses in life, but that was not the case in the jungle. In the boonies, it was every man for himself and that animus type law of survival was evident to all.

Socrates said, "Know thyself."

Leaders and followers would emerge unexpectedly from among us - irrespective of rank. Staying in touch with oneself was the key to survival and admitting you were one or the other was your passport into another day.

A lifetime would take place in the span of 30 minutes - increasing in intensity like the last few seconds of popcorn in the micro-wave or the "grand finale" of a fireworks extravaganza on the 4th of July.

How was I to know then that these "30 minute lifetimes" would become solid anchors that would hold me safe in the storms of my life 40 years down the road?

Insane, surreal experiences were the bill of fare every day - as it was in the crossing of a raging river with a company of grunts in early October.

It looked like the Niagara River in spring as its grayish-blue, cool water roared over the now-smooth boulders polished after centuries of grinding and tumbling while racing to the brink of the falls; but there we were again - being ordered by a follower in a leader's uniform.

The bed and sides of the river were rocky. The sizes of the rocks varied from huge boulders to garbage can size stones and then down to smooth pebbles on the bed (which were quite slippery). The gray water yielded to the reflections of the rocks beneath the surface and the sounds of the fury of the raging swells crashing against flat boulders - turning them smooth and rounded on the edges. Conversation was impossible. Our steel pots were being ripped off of our heads by the wind and all kinds of gear was floating downstream as we battled the current.

We were sticking the muzzle end of our M-16's into the river bed to try to get some footing as we crossed. We didn't even care if we fucked them up doing it. It was one of the most insane things we were ever ordered to do, but it was typical of the asshole leadership we were forced to contend with. It was this same piss-poor leadership that caused countless, meaningless loss of precious life.

I was roughly in the middle of our formation and midway across the river when we all watched an unknown face get caught by the current and go "ass over tea kettle" into a watery grave. He rolled down the river - bouncing off rocks and shedding his gear with every collision until he was out of sight. The sound of the water stifled our swearing and the water diluted our anger. Nobody knew who he was (which made the loss easier to take), but not to forget. This was the kind of fate we dabbled with in our minds, but sealed our lips to. I often imagined taking a direct hit from a B-40 or a RPG - or stepping on an anti-tank mine. Either fate would leave nothing to identify your remains – shit, they couldn't even find your dog tag at times.

This type of senseless loss furthered an ever-growing hatred and disrespect for officers who had ulterior motives that influenced their decisions. Some officers would avoid close contact and engage in no conversation with the grunts. The invisible wall was always there along with growing resentment and disgust - which we, the non-coms, made no effort to hide. When passing an officer, you simply put your head down and ignored their presence without a salute (which was an appreciated non-greeting for the smart ones and a punishable infraction to the dick heads).

The volatile relationships between blacks and whites demanded an effort all of its own too! The riots taking place back home spilled over onto the opposite side of our planet even though much effort was made to keep us ignorant of the news about the live ammo used at Kent State and other protests and demonstrations. My dad sent me newspapers telling about the riots in Detroit, Rochester, L.A., and all over the country. The Army couldn't keep it from us, so 1968 found us fighting off the Tet Offensive in the jungle - and back home, Americans were fighting the Racial Offensive in the cities throughout the USA. The learned behavior acquired at the dinner tables regarding racial issues was naturally suppressed in the states when walking the streets, but the jungle provided an arena without rules or laws. Survival still remained the most important issue on every days' agenda and depending on how you fit into each day, determined whether you would make it through the day or end up in a body bag - regardless of the color of your skin.

Racism, prejudice, bigotry, etc... were present, but painted on a different canvas. Survivors were color blind; actually every other social behavior along with it played second fiddle to survival.

It became effortless to violate your own conscience in life or death situations - which proved to be a redeeming quality for many and a sorrowful one for others.

We pick and choose where we go and who we go with at home, but Vietnam took us out of the comfort zone of home - forcing us to reckon with skewed thought patterns and altered belief systems that guided our destinies into lives of hatred and fighting without provocation. In Nam, all it took was the sharing of a cigarette - and all the deeply rooted anger, fear, bitterness, resentment and so on would melt away. A brief moment of eye contact would tell the tale and forecast who you could count on when the shit hit the fan. War makes strange bedfellows. Time was not available to test a relationship with anyone who did not share your skin color. A wink or a nod of the head would be the only gesture needed for a ride on the shoulders to an awaiting dust-off for a grunt who took a bullet in the gut.

Being a little older than everyone except my first Sergeant turned out to be an advantage as I had learned through experience some of the social skills needed to survive - regardless of where you were from back home.

Sergeant E-5 or "D," as we called him, did a tour with the 1st CAV before coming to the 4th Infantry. This particular day he was to lead a security detail through some of the thickest jungle we'd ever seen. Our path was actually an old road that hadn't been traveled on for many years. D was about 6'5", 200lbs and had a voice that carried for miles. He was a no-nonsense, natural born leader (with black skin) who hailed from Brooklyn (the 4th largest city in America), so he reminded us repeatedly. I liked him the first time we met, without any reason other than a gut instinct. I later discovered that the feeling was mutual.

We were to escort a 2½ ton truck with a Quad 50 cal. machine gun on its bed to a firebase about 4 klicks away. It was hot as hell and the rain was coming down in spurts.

A hand held mine sweeper was out in front of us along with me, the point man who was leading the escapade. The sound of the truck's roaring engine and spinning tires as they dipped into deep holes signaled a loud, telegraphed move for all to hear (if anyone was there to hear). So we all joined in with swearing at Charlie and singing along with the boom box maxed out on the volume.

We were warned that there were mines planted in the area (which added to the drama). I had the lead and I slowed our progress down because I was looking intently before I put my foot down on each step. The yelling from behind increased as the rest of the guys urged me to speed it up.

My right food missed an anti-tank mine by inches. The mine sweeper missed it by a mile, but the right front tire of the truck found it as it blew off the rim and dislodged the whole 8-cylinder engine off its mounts. The steam from the radiator filled the atmosphere and the fire from the explosion knocked us all down and away from the scene.

The voice of our Sarg pierced through it all as he commanded us to "kill the fuckin' dinks!"

We obliged as we fired in every direction. We didn't see anyone, but we knew they were there. Fire extinguishers quickly snuffed out the fire from the explosion, so all efforts were directed to the incoming small arms fire. The sound of AK-47's were everywhere. I popped in one clip after another - firing wildly at anything and everything.

I was standing next to the Sarg when Charlie threw a tin can grenade in between us. I hit the dirt and he picked me up by the seat of my pants and around my neck. I didn't know that most of the shrapnel from these crude grenades would fly close to the ground. He caught some on his legs, but I escaped without a mark. His wounds were small, but many (which we would discover later on).

That was the first time my life was saved by a black friend. We became close buddies, but he never let me forget how he saved my white ass. Now the next event proved to be one which would indelibly etch itself into my memory and remain forever.

The crew who manned the Quad 50 was with us on the trip, so they jumped up on the tilted bed of the truck, loaded up the four guns and began to fire. The jungle was falling down as if being cut with a huge weed whacker. Shell casings were flying everywhere. All the grunts on the ground stopped firing because there was no need. The two guys feeding the Quad-50 were popping open one box of ammo after another. The brass was flying everywhere. The gunner was sweeping back and forth, mowing down bamboo and trees as the smoke from the spent ammo engulfed the whole truck. What was left of the Viet-Cong ran for their lives - probably back home. The Quad 50 is an anti-aircraft weapon (not designed or intended for jungle use), but we proved them wrong that afternoon.

That Sergeant saved my life that day and the barriers between our races were brought down for all to see. This was an example to be played out for anyone who had the insight to pay attention and better their lives in regard to racial issues.

One thing was for sure, Charlie acquired a great deal of respect for a Quad 50 Cal. machine gun.

Conversely, there were days that would bring totally unexplainable eruptions of senseless cruelty. For example, our choppers would drop tens of thousands of pleas for surrender on pieces of paper called Chieu Hoi slips everywhere. Charlie would wave the slip in the air, shout Chieu Hoi, and surrender himself. This sounds very simple, but nothing was simple in Vietnam. So go, "the best laid plans of mice and men!"

The crap shoot was to gamble on who was sincere and who wasn't - because sometimes they had a bomb in a back pack which would go off as soon as they got close to you.

So, it was just another blistering hot afternoon when we finished filling our sandbags and constructing our perimeter when a NVA soldier popped out of the thick bush waving a slip and shouting "Chieu Hoi!" When he got about 20 feet away from us, our Lt. shot him with his M-16 and said: "I'm not in the mood for the fuckin' paperwork!"

And so it was just another day of meaninglessness death that ended with a little hot chow flown in as a reward for doing a good job.

Our Chieu-Hoi Charlie had nothing with him other than the slip of paper in his hand and an appetite. He was starving to death, but no one cared (especially the Lt. who zapped him).

At that moment a quote from a Robert Frost poem came to mind. "In three words I can sum up everything I've learned about life; it goes on." Except for Chieu-Hoi Charlie.

Convoys were to be avoided at all costs. They were, however, the means used to transport men and munitions as soon as the new major highways were laid between large cites. Trucks, tanks, and APC's were easy targets for RPG's, B-40 rockets, and even mortars. Overheating engines, flat tires and small arms fire from every direction in the dense jungle made for a nightmare experience every time we had the displeasure of going from point A to point B. Night time convoys were worse!

A five ton truck with a load of 4-deuce mortar rounds took a hit from an RPG and lit the sky around us for miles. Hours later, after cleaning up the mess, we took off again into the night.

The sky provided a show of stars that looked like a Christmas tree and the moon was so bright it almost felt warm. The air was cool and crisp - contaminated only by diesel fumes on an overnight trip from Pleiku to a huge firebase named the big "O" (oasis).

I was riding on top of a truckload of wooden foot lockers which were pinching my hands and butt no matter how I laid down or sat up due to the constant shifting and sliding. We finally hit a patch of smooth road and I dosed off into a dog tired sleep after finding some blankets which I used to make a cushion to lie on.

Something woke me up just as I was about to roll off the top of the truck. One leg and arm were dangling over the side and one more bounce would have dumped me into a ditch. I was alone that night and would not have been missed until morning. I came way too close to becoming another "'don't mean nothin'" story to the rest of the grunts.

We were approaching a large city and began to creep along at about 5 miles an hour or so. The locals were selling food, drinks and trinkets. Hundreds of little kids and old women lined the road into the city and they were selling everything - including themselves. A GI in the truck in front of me bought an ice cold bottle of coke from an old lady who had a canvas bag filled with beer, cokes and ice. A few days later we heard he died of intestinal bleeding. The coke was laced with ground glass.

It became obvious that no one could be trusted - young or old, man, woman or child.

The barber who cut our hair in the base camp during the day was the sapper who was throwing satchel charges into the fuel depot at night. A few weeks later we were on another convoy when we saw an old lady selling ice cold cokes out of a canvas bag. A bunch of us threw cans of food at her as we went by at 20 MPH. I watched her drop to her knees and then down to the ground as the whole convoy of G.I.'s peppered her broken, bloody body with cans and rocks.

Six months in country erased the option of when (and when not) to shoot, but 6 months also gave birth to the new meaning for the word "SHORT."

Short meant you were past 6 months in country and when you were "real short," you became "NEXT." Next meant you were just days away from a plane ride home. When you greeted someone, you would just shout 15 or 7 or 21, the other guy would do the same, bragging about exactly how many days he had remaining in country. This would invoke great laughter and verbal debates - and when you hit single digits, it was, "I'm not short, I'm next, mother fucker!"

I can't say when, how, or why, but I began to wake up in the morning and remain asleep - walking out into the day in a trance-like, numb state of existence.

I was accustomed to daydreaming about thoughts of home and my job as a sheet metal worker, but these thoughts began to fade away - creating space for a new set of memories of body bags, burning villages, old ladies selling ground glass and an endless stream of asshole 2nd lieutenants.

Each day of new memories became the rationale for the future days of existence. My life back home was being erased off the paper except for the light indentations underneath on the pad of my past. I was disappearing and I knew it!

After being in country and in the field for about 8 months, it became obvious that we were all acting without a script, some even trying to portray characters we had seen in war movies. The impressions formed by the silver screen of heroes or cowards became the characters we would audition for and act out as if we earned the part. Nobody was real! None of us in real life would dare to do the things we were commanded to do; so the escape was to act, to pretend you were someone else. Then you wouldn't feel bad about what you did because you knew that soon you would walk off the stage and allow yourself to feel again and be a real person who cares and loves.

Of course there were some who refused to act. They would simply go nuts in the middle of a firefight, grab a tree and cry for their mommy. Crying for "mommy" happened a lot, especially from the big tough guys who acted like John Wayne when nothing was happening. I discovered the same phenomenon 40 years later while listening to old men brag about what brave heroes they were in Vietnam - only to find out after the second cup of coffee at Starbucks that they were never in a firefight, had never seen the enemy, or never fired one round during a year in country. Empty wagons make a lot of noise!

It wasn't a matter of how much you could take, it was about how much you could act, play the part, and pretend it wasn't really you who was shooting people.

I heard Jack Lemon on "Inside the Actor's Studio" with James Lipton saying that actors have got to remember to not cross the line when portraying the life of someone else. He was very sober and serious when describing his preparations to act out the life of another. He said it was a very dangerous thing. He was right!

Another phenomenon was that of being able to spot the guys who would never "go home" - even if they went home. Dabbling with the fleeting horror of being drawn into that vortex yourself, was the ultimate of all fears. A simple act of kindness like giving little kids chocolate or smiling at a pregnant girl and pointing to her big belly became welcome life lines which were there for the taking if you wanted to hang on to your dissolving life.

A very old Papa San in Kontum insisted that my squad spend the night in the front yard of his house in the city. He never stopped smiling or talking. He brought out a very old bottle of whiskey and insisted we all toast to whatever - it didn't matter, we just raised our glasses and drank. Then we all ate rice, laughed, and pointed to each other while trying to communicate across the language barrier. Understanding each other was not the issue; it was about the freedom to enjoy life. That was why we were there - and in that moment of time, we all knew it. I wrote home about that evening in Kontum and my Dad submitted it to the Buffalo Evening News. They printed the whole story in a "letters from Vietnam" editorial section. I kept this newspaper clipping on the wall of my office for over 40 years. It read:

> *My battalion had the mission of helping to clean some communist troops out of Kontum. Because of the intense fighting, it was impossible for a while to resupply us and our outfit was short of food for several days.*
>
> *The inhabitants of Kontum learned of our needs and invited us to eat in their homes. I couldn't speak a*

word of their language nor they of mine, but hunger is a universal condition.

Everywhere I went in Kontum I was greeted with a smile and a bottle of beer. I ate like a king and I guess I'll never know where they got that beer.

Do you know why I was greeted that way, Mr. Demonstrator? Well, we pushed the Viet Cong out of Kontum and the people have freedom they never knew existed. This is why the US is in South Vietnam. – PFC Kenneth Kinsler, Buffalo, NY

I told everyone that I didn't want them to come to the airport to see me off. I didn't want to say goodbye, but I wanted to go. I needed to go. I had to go. I needed to find out who I was and I thought it might just happen in Vietnam.

My divorce came in June, my draft notice in July, and my 26th birthday in August. The timing was incredibly close, badly synchronized, but whatever. If my draft notice had come 26 days later, I would have been exempt. I guess I could blame my Mom and Dad for that - just like all the other bad things happening to me back then that were someone else's fault. I was a quintessential finger pointer back home, but now I was using an M-16. I tried to rid myself of anger, hatred, bitterness, and self-pity by using hand grenades, machine guns, M-79's, claymores, and knives. But killing other people was not ridding me of personal pain.

My girlfriend took me to the airport. I didn't want my mom or dad or anyone else to see me off. My girlfriend was the only relationship I felt I knew or was comfortable with. I even asked her to lie to me if she found someone else... and she did. I didn't trust anyone - not even myself. My "replacement" was one of my good friends, but she lied really good, all year, and even sent me a birthday cake. The bakery guaranteed delivery anywhere in Vietnam in perfect condition - and they did it, even in the rain. None of us could believe it. We keep in touch now from a distance, 46 years after the cake. When I came home, she couldn't face me, so we conversed through messages given to her mother. I had a few beers with my friend who married her. I shook his hand and told him I wasn't pissed off, just glad I made it home in one piece, but that story might be in my next book.

Back then, way back then, before the Army, I didn't much care about anyone except for me. I had a 7 year old son, an ex-wife, Mom and Dad and two girlfriends. I also had a great job (which paid well) and a host of good friends.

None of them mattered now. I sold my car and gave everything else away. I put $180.00 in my pocket and said goodbye to my whole life as I walked up the ramp of the 707.

Little did I know, I would never come home. Nothing would ever be the same. I flew back to the states one year later, but I didn't "arrive." My life came to an end in the jungle, leaving me with an existence of hooking one day to the next without being shot at or worrying about stepping on a mine. New crazy habits developed as I always had to sit facing the entrance doors of restaurants. I now had to ask people to sit on my right side because I'm deaf in my left ear. Sure, there is life after war, but with a different definition for the word, LIFE.

What took place in one day of Nam would be enough to fill a 300 page book. The nightmares of one small arms firefight could be a screen writer's dream. Words cannot describe it, the psyche cannot grasp it, pictures fail to show it and the mind will shut it down, turn it off, or blank it out if need be.

So the consequences of deciding to get up and go through another day result in searching for a reason why you came home at all - because nothing fits together anymore. I still find myself trying to reconnect the dots. 46 years have passed and I feel I'm still staring at a puzzle.

War brings out the best and worst in people – we can choose to examine or ignore this fact. We never really push ourselves to the max mentally or physically, so we never find out what we're capable or incapable of.

Not being in control of our insides was more devastating than the external minutia of life - then and now - and that's just another one of the crippling aspects of Nam. The things we can see are difficult to cope with, but things inside us erupt without warning. Blind spots triggered by a little smoke from a burning log or a car back firing still lurch me up off my seat.

We do and say things when we're drunk that we deny when recounted by our drinking buddies the next day. The same held true of firefights. We would talk about what happened as if we didn't actually do any of it. This also allowed us to eat a meal while smelling rotten flesh and ignore the drying blood in between our fingers which caused them to stick together like some kind of carpenter's glue.

We became immoral machines without hearts, protecting the treasures of goodness and kindness, guarding over them, never revealing their whereabouts to anyone including ourselves.

One of my best friends was called Jersey because, of course, he hailed from New Jersey. He liked to cut the ears off dead gooks and make a necklace out of them. The smell would go away after a week or so. He broke all the rules and never wore a shirt so he got sunburned all the time, but he never stopped laughing and joking.

He was 6'4" and had as much hair on his chest and beard as he did on his head. He looked like a bear and he ate like a horse. His laughter was contagious. He was the guy you wanted to be next to when the shit hit the fan in a bar fight back home.

When we got into a firefight, he would burn up his M-16 - firing one clip after another until it would seize up. Then he would throw grenades and scream - calling Charlie every kind of motherfuckerrrrrr under the sun.

We became buddies instantly since we both had the whole Yankee thing in common. He never showed any fear of anything (which was another contagious condition). He volunteered to walk point and didn't wait for orders from a Lt. to do what needed to be done – especially when it was obvious.

We both had about 6 months in country when we climbed up hill 684 at Chu Moor Mountain in Kontum Province.

Instant respect and awe was given to anyone with 684 written on their helmet cover. Guys would look at the number, then look down and away from the eyes of anyone who survived. It was an embarrassment to our generals and colonels, but not to the NVA. It was a brilliant piece of strategy never before used - at least not on us, up to that point in time.

If you walked into an "L" shaped ambush, there was no safe direction to run - and we all feared them, but 684 was different and even more devastating than an ambush. It was brilliant. It baffled our brass and at a cost of life and limb never to be equaled in my tour of duty.

Most memories can be managed with time and therapy, but 684 is the exception. That mountain carved a mental scar into the minds of all who miraculously survived.

Before I attempt to write about 684, I should insert here what happened after 684 (which proved to be an unprecedented event not to be equaled as well).

Up to now, this endeavor of writing the memoirs of my tour in Vietnam has been an experience I've longed to accomplish for years, but writing about 684 brought an unexpected halt in my endeavor. Language cannot convey certain events in life from one person to another regardless of their command or skill with the written word.

Poets, song writers and painters tell us more from their hearts than our best efforts with words - so then, why try to write about such horror? I do not have the answer, but I truly believe that the 684's of war have a need to be spoken of, seen on the silver screen, and read about in books. Why are we so taken with writings on the walls deep inside the pyramids?

Maybe venting will be healthy for me – or maybe this will fall into the hands of some young soldier before he goes into battle.

Anyway, after a two month hiatus from writing and many long and thoughtful deliberations, I'm going to give it a shot (pardon the pun).

There's a caveat to the telling of 684, which to this day has me baffled, but it must be shared. The media in 1968, as it is today, was motivated by a questionable set of limitations or protocols.

Without "intentionally" trying to shock would-be viewers, there were occasions when live footage of actual battles were televised and the folks at home would actually see it in their living rooms - uncut accounts of their loved ones fighting or being carried onto a helicopter minus a leg or an arm. Maybe it was intentional, but that's another story.

Never-the-less, ABC's cameras were there the day we went up and the day we got off 684.

With that in mind, an Army-colored olive drab Chevy sedan pulled into the driveway of 67 Wyoming Ave in the latter part of an April morning in 1968. My Mom fell down crying on the back porch. Two officers knocked on the door. They were greeted by my dad (who was also shedding tears by this time). The officers quickly shook dad's hand and told him not to be upset because they were the bearers of good news. They told him that I survived a great battle which lasted four days and that I had sustained only very minor wounds and that Gen. S himself had decorated me and my buddies in the field right after the battle ended. My dad got drunk on shots and beers, and my mom told everyone in the city about her son. The Buffalo Evening News printed the story of 684 and that day ended with mom and dad crying and laughing out of joy and pride. BUT... My mom could have suffered a heart attack! So much for Protocol!

Where do I start? What I'm about to share with you was thoroughly reviewed by the Army, so I heard, and to my knowledge, the mistake was never made again.

Chapter 4
684

Knowing our patterns of operation, Charlie devised a fool proof battle plan. The NVA (North Vietnamese Army) chose a particular mountain - not too high and not connected by a ridge line to any other mountain. It must have taken months to prepare the maneuver. They dug in un-noticeable positions all around the mountain, but none on top and none at the base either.

They knew our standard procedure was to hump a few klicks, go to the top of any mountain and dig in for the night. They knew we might stay a few days while running patrols and then move on to another location and repeat everything. So they allowed us to climb up to the top of 684, passing right by them and not firing a shot. They remained totally un-noticed and we simply dug in as usual and got prepared on we thought was just another mountain in the central highlands. Charlie also knew about the "mad minute." After digging in for the night and before setting out our claymores just before the sun went down, we would open fire for one minute - drenching the whole perimeter with our M-16's. Then we would do a little shouting before settling down for a good night's sleep in the moonlight.

It was rumored that no one had set foot on this hill for at least 400 to 500 years. There were no trails in the bush and none of our bombs had destroyed the first tree.

The silence of the morning was shattered by the wisp of the first B-40 rocket - then the second, then the third, and fourth. Then the entire dense jungle surrounding our perimeter lit up like a fucking Christmas tree with muzzle flashes and streams of tracers in every direction. The thumping of mortars was endless. This kind of firepower would traditionally last a couple minutes, but not this morning.

We knew we had to return fire or face the risk of being overrun. So fire we did. I could actually hear Jersey over the deafening sound of all the shooting. His defiant shouting "come on mother fuckers" left us all with renewed confidence.

Then it all stopped just as abruptly as it started. The smell of spent ammo wafted into my nose to a degree that I had never experienced! My M-16 was hot and about ready to seize-up. The M-60 next to me was smoking and the two guys who manned it were dead. The radios took over and dominated the once peaceful atmosphere. Trying to figure out what had just happened was secondary to dealing with what remained of a full company of Infantry.

A situation report was sent in by our commander's RTO followed by our first sleepless night on 684.

We could not get our dead or wounded out because Charlie closed up the circle around us after we walked past him. We were too close to the enemy in every direction to move a muscle or be helped by artillery. Helicopters could not land; they would just fly by to drop off ammo and food, but took a lot of hits doing it - and some went down trying. We could not get out and nobody could get in, so we became ducks in a shooting gallery. All of our body bags were full, and many more soldiers were dying from bleeding to death. This was getting tough to take for the medics who were still alive.

The radios continued to flood the air around us and our desperation intensified because we could all monitor the dialog since we were so close to each other. This was not supposed to happen to us. We were the Americans here. We had all the firepower, planes, aircraft carriers and bombs! But Charlie had us by the balls and he knew it. The NVA had total control. Headquarters decided to send up some help to break their hold on us or cut a hole in their perimeter and allow us to get off the top of 684. Charlie killed or wounded them all in their attempt. None of this was in your local newspaper, needless to say.

After the second day, we could not sit up to shit or piss, so we did it lying down - in our pants. The smell of spent ammo gave way to new odors of vomit, shit, piss, fear - and of course, the humming of the flies (which sounded like an overloaded circuit breaker in a 400 amp load center).

Night and day would bring brief firefights lasting 10 to 15 minutes. The unspoken facts were that Charlie was too afraid to rush us because he knew we still had plenty of ammo and enough men to drop him in his tracks if he tried to come up to the top of the hill. And we were not about to quit - knowing that somehow, some way, we would eventually over power the NVA.

No training can prepare a warrior for this kind of situation. Text books and DR manuals should at least pre-warn or make an attempt at what cannot be explained with a lesson manual for battlefield procedure, not that it would prepare anyone, but an acknowledgement of the unknown would be a worthy point to be pondered in Army training classrooms. Oh well!

We were practically sitting in each other's laps, so it was decided to make an attempt at spreading out and gaining a bit more real estate. Our 2nd Lt. (who was the best we ever had), volunteered a squad of 6 of us for the mission. We got about 30 feet out from our position before being noticed by Charlie. The Lt. was in the lead and found a very wide tree for cover before Charlie pinned him down. He couldn't move away from the tree. He couldn't move a muscle without being sprayed with bullets. It was the same tactic all over again, only in miniature form. When would we learn!?

We could see the muzzle flashes so we devised a plan. We put our guns on semi-auto and laid down a consistent field of cover fire with two shooting and three re-loading, then three shooting and two re-loading. Charlie kept his head down while our Lt. crept back to us and we all returned to the top of hill 684.

One of our guys got some shrapnel in his lung which caused him to spit blood, but other than that, we all made it back alive - especially our favorite Lt.

One of the guys in my platoon on 684 possessed the uncanny ability to fear absolutely nothing. He blatantly ignored bullets whizzing by him and would simply sit on his helmet and eat right in the middle of a firefight. He had a great sense of humor. He joked about everything - and if you didn't know him well, you would swear he was kind of enjoying himself. No one ever witnessed him getting excited about anything. He was from California, which would explain the major portion of his unusual behaviors (sorry it's just me), but he was liked by everyone - black, white, and Latino, and he was respected by all the officers who knew him.

One day we passed by a shallow creek that was about a foot deep and 20 feet wide and had a bed of small, smooth stones. California put on his birthday suit and was the first to take a dip. Within two minutes of watching him lying in the cool water, our whole squad followed suit and jumped in. We broke out the soap and enjoyed that beautiful clean, clear water as thousands of people had done previously for centuries before us. In that brief moment of bliss, he created for us the ability to enjoy life at the moment we were living it.

Early in the afternoon on the third day of our stay on 684, there was a lull in activity - which created a suspicion evidenced by the look on all our faces (except of course California's). The silence was deafening as it eased us into a sense of false security; thinking it might be over, and worst of all, getting off the edge a little bit. We referred to that as "half steppin'". You have to realize that there was a language understood only by those who had been in country for a number of months. It was a unique mixture of Cajun, Ebonics, Vietnamese, Redneck and Yankee. In Nam, this was the language that was used for humor and instruction alike. Here's a little example: "Looka here dude, Charlie catch you half-steppin', he will bring serious pee on yo ass, put you in a ma fuckin' bag back to da world, Holmes." Crazy, huh?

At any rate, our "California Dreamer" was sitting on his helmet eating while all the rest of us were lying down or half into our bunkers when the whiz of a B-40 rocket demolished our quiet afternoon. The impact followed the whiz by several seconds which told us that Charlie was a good distance away - and that was the only good part of the day. My next thought took an eternity to reveal itself.

I had lost my vision. In its place was a red or rosy colored world where I could not distinguish anything. My hearing (or lack thereof) could only be likened to my previous boat ride experience into the gorge at the bottom of Niagara Falls. The noise of the falling water was so loud that you could not hear any other sounds of any kind.

I felt someone shove me into the bottom of my little bunker. I then began coughing uncontrollably. The air around us was filled with dirt and dust which was suffocating everyone who was still breathing. Then I realized how fortunate I was to still be breathing.

I began to hear faint voices after a few minutes, but they sounded far away and I couldn't quite figure that out. Then I started to see shadows, but the redness was thicker which made everything obscure.

"You're gonna be ok, stay down" was the first discernable thing I heard. I was thankful that it was the voice of our Lt.

The shooting subsided and was replaced with moans, cries and screaming from everyone except of course California whose back looked like a freshly cut sirloin steak. Hundreds of tiny pieces of shrapnel had torn the shirt off his back, revealing large and small cuts from shoulder to waist. The rockets impact was about 10 feet to the rear of us all. None of us were spared from wounds.

The guy who was sitting facing California had his nose cut off as cleanly as if performed by a surgeon. We all had cuts here and there from the shrapnel - and out of the midst of all the chaos, California's first comment was, "I'm going back to the world, dude!"

A foreign thought was spreading itself through our minds, smothering our confidence and arrogance. It didn't show up in our speech, but it was there and the fear of not getting off this hill alive metastasized like a cancer in all of us.

My eyesight and hearing bounced back, and along with it a strong, deep pain in my left ear. This ear ache turned out to become my lifelong souvenir from hill 684.

The imminent threat of being overrun became the single topic of discussion by all due to our dwindling manpower and Charlie's awareness of a diminishing firepower from the summit.

In order to thwart Charlie's plan to rush us, it was decided to let the mountain know that it would be a big mistake. We accomplished this by firing our M-79's and machine guns in every direction with only short breaks in between for hours at a time. One thing we had was plenty of ammo. It seemed to work, but we knew about Charlie's psychological tactics

- or some of them anyway. What none of us understood was that the NVA were fighting for their country; we were fighting to go home. Our fight was 365 days long, his was a lifetime. We won if we got to go home, he was home, and was not going to quit until we were all home - or dead. The nobility of going to war for a cause bigger than oneself was his edge - his constant advantage.

Fighting for yourself is like a prize fight, a boxing match - and the winning prize is that you get a ticket home. They were willing to die for their country. We didn't even care who won - as long as we got to go home.

It was now four days into the battle on hill 684 and our mental strength was depleted.

We started receiving incoming small arms fire, so Jersey and I opened up with our M-79 grenade launchers.

We were two bunkers apart so we covered a broad field of fire. He would shoot a round with me ducking down, then I would send one out and he would duck down. We kept it up for 15 to 20 minutes, taking only brief breaks and then cranking it up again. I got confused and shot off a round at the same time he was up, so some of the shrapnel from my M-79 hit him. He called me every kind of "mother fucker" under the sun - laughing all the time. "It ain't enough I gotta put up with fuckin dinks, now I got Kinsler shootin' me!" he shouted.

Everybody on the hill was laughing - except Charlie. Then it happened... Jersey took a direct hit from a B-40 rocket and simply disappeared. There was no trace of him anywhere. Nothing remained to identify him.

Someone pushed me off the diving board. The loss of control was welcomed and turned into a relief - until I felt the sting of two strong slaps on my face, knocking me down. It was my Lt. He saw it happen, and he knew I was checking out because of what happened to Jersey. Intuitively, the Lt. knew I might not return, so he made the decision to try and bring me back. Luckily for me, he did. With some strong slaps on the face, the Lt brought me back to a world of sanity, or reality, or feelings, or whatever this place is that we all stumble through.

"Don't mean nothin'" wasn't working too effectively on this situation as we talked about Jersey many times like they talked about Cool Hand Luke after he died.

"That Luke was a world changer" said George Kennedy - and so was Jersey.

We all died a little bit with Jersey that day, but memories of him kept us alive. He changed everyone who knew him and his sacrifice gave us a reason to carry on. It was a wakeup call, a shift into overdrive. The fear of us all dying was overwhelming, but was trumped by the need to go on and at least avenge Jersey's death, if nothing else.

Finally the F-111's cut a wedge out of the circle of the NVA surrounding us. It wasn't overly wide, but it was enough for those of us who remained to vacate the top of the hill.

Carrying our wounded forced us to move slowly on our retreat, so we were given orders to follow a plan which worked surprisingly well.

We got in line and descended one by one with myself and a First Lt. being the last to check out. He had a radio and different colored smoke grenades and I had as many hand grenades as I could carry. He would throw a smoke grenade to our rear which would be identified by a chopper that was making passes perpendicular to our direction of descent. Meanwhile, I was throwing one grenade after another while walking backwards to keep Charlie off our ass. Between the choppers, mini guns and rockets along with my hand grenades, we managed to get down from 684 with a measure of dignity and a newfound respect for our enemy.

We were getting close to the bottom of our mountain of misery at Chu Moor when our 105's were getting too close for comfort as they were called upon to provide cover fire for our descent. A large piece of shrapnel cut the right leg off my buddy K right at the knee. I gave the rest of my grenades to the First Lt. and picked up K with a fireman's carry over my right shoulder. He was "mother fucking Charlie" without a stop. His leg was dangling with just a narrow piece of skin holding it from falling off. He grabbed it - trying to rip it off. Now he was "mother fucking" his leg, saying he didn't need this God damn leg and on and on. I told him they'd sew it back on, but he ripped it off and threw it away. I was using my left hand to squeeze his veins, trying to slow down the bleeding as we were getting close to a dust-off chopper at the bottom of 684. Thanks or no thanks to the internet, I found out 46 years later that he died on the way to the hospital.

Well, for whatever it's worth, K was a black kid and one of my best friends. You will understand why I made that comment later on.

If one learns to speak Latin, it becomes easy to take on Italian, Spanish or French - and so it was with life after hill 684. Well maybe not easy, but doable.

What are the things that made us happy or cause us to survive or just get up and go for it one more day? God only knows, but we all got a dose of that something that kept us going on 684, and we broke a major rule talking about Jersey for months to come.

Thirty of us died in four days on that hill with close to five times that number being wounded, but every one of us who was there left a piece of our life that's still there today.

Chapter 5
TET Offensive

For the most part, life was boring up until Vietnam. We get jobs and think about returning to the same work place or office for 25 years and find ourselves wrapped up in a sequence of events so predictable and uneventful that the passion for everyday life turns into tasteless manna. Holidays become the only interruption to the monotony and even they have a way of getting sucked into the quagmire of the calendar.

If nothing else, a year in Nam provided a renewed lifelong appreciation for clean sheets and air-conditioning and an unquenchable thirst for the boring everyday tasks like mowing the lawn and doing the dirty dishes, of all things. Who would have guessed?

"Cultivation to the mind is as necessary as food to the body" - Cicero

Predictability and routine disappeared when the TET Offensive broke out. We were on a merry-go-round of chaos. The Brass was caught totally off guard and all their long and short term plans were trashed.

For our Generals, it must have been like riding a bicycle for the first time. I'd be willing to bet that West Point didn't, or couldn't, prepare the Brass for what the NVA had in store for us during the TET offensive.

Our offense turned to defense in one minute - catching us off guard as everyone was scrambling to stay alive, regardless of where you were in Vietnam.

Ships at sea, planes in the air and all the might of our bombs cannot help or even support ground troops when your enemy decides to turn the fight into a hand to hand battle. All you have is what's on your back because support is cut off, planes are on the ground, ships at sea are silent, and everybody was scared shitless.

Charlie decided he had enough of this bull crap and the strength of his determination was seen on our faces as we sat at the end of an airport runway waiting for our choppers to arrive. We were scared. Everybody was scared when the TET broke out!

Nothing was mundane about this life! The adrenalin was pumping, the scuttle butt was spreading like cancer through a body - with a message of World War III.

Earlier that month, we took a hard fought hill and discovered many Chinese troops. The color of their uniforms and weapons were distinctively different and a red light lit up on all our dashboards. The puzzle was taking shape and revealing a future none of us wanted to see.

The entire city of Kontum had been taken over by the NVA. We were assigned to take it back. As usual, no other details! Then suddenly, something new was added to the landscape. Priests and ministers were walking down the runway on both sides and there were several of them - more than I had ever seen in one place at one time.

Choppers were coming in by the dozens, hauling away hundreds of us off to the outskirts of Kontum.

Memories of the huge Catholic Church I attended as a boy flirted with my thinking and ushered in a welcomed pause in the momentum of the day.

The buses I rode as a boy in Buffalo had cords strung along the top of the windows and when you pulled them, the driver would stop and let you exit. So I pulled the metaphorical cord as the priest approached me. I could see the fear in his eyes as he was more interested in seeing to it that he would be able to see everyone rather than zeroing in on the one he was talking to. Of course, he had no idea I had just gotten off the bus. So there we were trying to fix everything in two minutes that had I fucked up in a lifetime - and also get me properly prepared for my eminent change of dimension.

He was a short, fat, freckled faced man of the cloth who was doing it all by the numbers. "When was your last confession, son? Are you married? Are you divorced? Are you seeing anyone at home? Is she a Catholic girl? Do you plan to marry her if you make it back?" He half-heartedly inquired.

I sat stoic, but reflective as I bit my lip. "Father, How about my sins? I want you to hear my confession!"

Freckle Face had no interest in hearing my confession. He cut me off and said "Son, I can't hear your confession because you're divorced and if you marry that girl, she will be ex-communicated from the Church."

"But Father, what about my sins?" I pleaded.

All he said was "Sorry, son" and he moved on to the next guy.

To that end, I "jumped back on the bus," and rejoined the people who were in touch with life and themselves.

The roar of the choppers was intensifying but they did not muffle out my telling that no-good Freckle Faced priest to "go fuck himself!" Then I pointed up to the sky, shouting "and fuck you too!"

And they wonder why we're not the same when we come home. A military machine that can't help you, a God who rejects you, and people who spit on you in the airport when you get home. But the decisions are still always there; whether to succumb to the surprises of life, ignore them or allow them to become the genesis of resources that will mold us into who we actually are. I opted to use, in a positive way, what could have crippled me for life that day and I turned it into a token that afforded me a very long bus ride in my life to come - with the assurance that God did not reject me because of what I was doing or had done in Nam and that life goes on in spite of what anyone says to you.

The time for religious drama came to an abrupt end when we saw a shrimp boat chopper with a cargo net full of dead bodies coming in. They didn't have time to put them in body bags, so the arms and legs were sticking out through the nylon netting. We were going where they were coming from, but it really didn't matter. It was just another fucking day in South Vietnam.

The ruts in the road in front of my home in the winter time grew so deep that if your front tires found themselves in the right turning curve, you made a right turn even if you wanted to go straight. The ice was so thick it was unbelievable - and so were February's turn of events in Vietnam.

It was one chopper ride after another. A change without a choice, a trip without traveling - ushering you into a future you'd live out all alone. With the ruts came a freeing sensation; from a life lived, to a life ending, to a life without a past or a destination, a loneliness not effected by time or space, without interruptions. Just like a February in Buffalo, trying to go straight, but being forced to turn left or right, no matter what you do, one day hooked itself to the next like a freight train being guided by rail switches - screaming its way through the middle of a city in the dark of night.

You get a free pass in Nam for the rest of your life because no one can judge you, how did the song go?

"I am a rock, I am an Island and a rock feels no pain and an island never cries." Thank you Simon and Garfunkel!

So now it was going to be street fighting - something totally new for us. Up until now, it was fighting in jungles amid never ending mountains - up and down, up and down.

This was more like the movies of WWII we have all seen - we even got to work with tanks and APC's (which gave us a quasi-sense of security), but tanks were easy targets to hit, so there was a down side. There was always a down side.

The tide of the war had once again changed back to how it was. Charlie couldn't sustain the TET offensive because of weak supply lines. Now and then they would try to hold the ground they gained, but in the end of every battle, our factories and logistics were the victors - just as it was in WWII.

It was the hot season. Not a drop of rain was in the forecast. The buildings around us cut off whatever breeze was available. The stone, glass and metal of the city transitioned from mountain greenery into an Italian pizza oven – radiating blistering heat that hurt your eyes and burnt your uncovered skin. The smell of death was everywhere.

Our push was so strong that Charlie had to leave his dead behind. The stench of the dead bodies emanated into the air and destroyed our daydreams of that bread coming out of the pizza parlor oven. I saw footage of the death camps in WWII and it looked like that, but the foul odors forced the acids to churn whatever was in my stomach into vomit, thus demanding that I swallow hard and fast. The cameras in my eyes respond to the rewind button to this day. The savagery of war or man's inhumanity to fellow man leaped off the silver screen onto a live stage that afternoon without intermissions.

It was so strange to see soccer fields with crude little bleachers and refreshment stands, commercial stores that sold carpets from Turkey or Iraq, and furniture cheap and expensive alike. There were sidewalk cafes and even a movie theater. If you stretched your imagination, it almost looked a little like back home.

The stores had folding steel curtains or corrugated metal doors with heavy duty locks and all the merchandise was left undisturbed.

Interesting foreign smells of incense, restaurant kitchens, musty furniture and vacant workshops filled the air around us. We were approaching a huge outdoor food market area (which provided a new set of aromas) to counteract the stench of the dead bodies that were blowing up like balloons lying everywhere around us. Some of them had their penises cut off and stuck in their mouths. As we walked down the street, we noticed that on both sides were ditches which served as sewers and drainage, but now were crying for rain.

A jeep full of Aussies with their fancy hats and chrome plated AK-47's were coming toward us.

They were all laughing, calling us Yanks, and enjoying the madness of the moment when suddenly a trail of machine gun bullets began to hit the road behind the jeep. The Aussies began weaving like a snake as the bullets chased their jeep from behind, getting closer and closer with each round. They shifted into high gear and disappeared in a cloud of smoke and dust leaving us to become the new targets.

The bouncing bullets were coming toward me and some of us were returning fire, but their gun was far away and the multi-storied buildings had hundreds of windows, so none of us were sure where to shoot or where to go to get out of his sights. I opted to jump into a ditch - which to my dismay, was already occupied by a gook who was about ready to explode after lying there dead for days. I rolled over him to avoid incoming bullets, and sure enough, he popped! I was ready to swallow a couple of bullets myself right then when I began to hear the only cure that always pulled us through.

Laughter! My buddies were laughing hysterically and I joined them while I was vomiting. My shirt and pants were saturated with rotten body fluids and no change of clothes was available, so nobody would get near me.

Somebody finally took out the gook with the gun, so we headed down the street where I found a water well with a hand-pump. I stripped down and washed myself and my clothes as best I could. That story was told over and over to every new guy that came in and relived and retold during every lull we had.

Our mission was quite simple, move through the city, block by block, house by house, push out the NVA and give it back to the people.

I worked with a three man team. The first guy would kick in the door the second guy would throw in a grenade; the last guy would run in and spray the room with his M-16. We destroyed a lot of good furniture and didn't find anyone stupid enough to hang around. Their tactic was to use their snipers in the rear of their retreat. They did this to antagonize us while slowing down our advance. We would spend all day trying to get one gook perched on top of a thick, tall, tree while hundreds of NVA troops were escaping back into the jungle.

It was a conundrum never to be solved. A war that was unwinnable. An MO (modus operandi) not found in the libraries of West Point. A season that would never end for a generation of 19 year old fine young men who would spend the rest of their lives in recovery - and their loved ones back home in awe, unable to keep from shaking their heads and saying, "He just wasn't the same when he came home."

The prospect of working with tanks was a welcome change. We walked alongside at a snail's pace and learned how to ignore the bullets ricocheting off the steel – all the while knowing that the turret was about to turn in the direction of the fire and soon the blast of the big gun would silence the atmosphere of the annoying AK's.

At night we would set up at an intersection of streets. The grunts would bunk down in the ditches and watch the tracers fly by in every direction - waking up only when they would bounce off a nearby tank.

We were working in conjunction with the South Vietnamese Army who were issued APC's and jeeps with 50 cal. machine guns.

Our tank commander told our interpreter to instruct the South Vietnamese to set up to our right at the next intersection, about 500 feet away. They were also instructed to be sure to never shoot in our direction during the night - no matter what was going on. Communication was one of our big problems with the South Vietnamese, so the T.C. (tank commander) made sure everyone understood the plan for the night, in spades.

The sun hadn't gone down but an hour before we were receiving 50 cal. and small arms fire from our right. The screaming on the radios started and the firing stopped. An hour or so later, it started up again. Then we heard the tanks engines crank up, the turret turned to our right and fired one round down the street to our right. We all enjoyed a quiet nights rest after the fires went out.

I paid little attention to the historic Vietnam I was walking in every day.

Statues of De Galle were found in the strangest places - monasteries, mosques and temples were everywhere and the Catholic presence was the strongest of all.

My wife and I went to a church one night some 20 years after coming home and an elderly man, who was well respected there, told my wife that I had been in and among people and places of great evil and that curses were spoken over my life.

He had never met me before and it was the first time we had ever gone to that church - and it was the last time as well. I shall refrain from comment about curses and the like, except to say that I personally do not put a great deal of stock in them.

We were approaching a large open sort of a court yard area. The smell of spent ammo indicated a freshly fought battle - not by the forward element of my company, but by those who came through in the morning before our arrival - or so we thought. There were lots of dead bodies, but there was a weirdness in the atmosphere – kind of like Déjà vu. We thought our guys kicked ass here, but we found out it was the retreating NVA killing the civilians. They believed the local people were helping us, and some of them were, so they were all killed by the retreating NVA or VC.

Talk about confusion! So in the middle of all this, a monk priest walks up to the middle of the courtyard, kneels down and pours gasoline on his head and body and lights himself up. A gesture of sacrifice for peace to his God (so we were told). He moved not one muscle as the flames disintegrated his body into ashes for all to see. It was time to eat and move on. Just another day in Nam.

Who would expect to see a good old fashioned liquor store, fully stocked? Yours truly found it! We filled our back packs with the best cognac money could buy, knowing the hangovers were going to get our minds off our heartaches - at least for a little while.

I got a fresh set of clothes and we continued down the yellow brick road - brainless and heartless, but with plenty of courage.

One of my buddies was a virgin. He had led a sheltered, simple life back home. He was a church goer who lived in the hills of wherever. We were good friends and he was a good soldier with a big dumb heart. I told him to make sure to use a rubber when he decided which one of the old skanks that came by on an overloaded Lambretta would be his first sexual experience. He came into my hooch about a week later wanting to show me his penis. It was as red as a firecracker, swollen twice its size and it "hurt real bad to pee" as he put it.

They shipped him to the Philippines and was not allowed to return home for the rest of his life. Names had not yet been given to the strains of V.D. in Vietnam, so we were told.

I looked around one morning and realized that all but a very few of my buddies that I had when I got in country were still there. I suddenly felt very lonely and wondered what they were thinking about me - or if they were thinking about me at all - or if anyone was even capable of thought about anything.

We were becoming wind-up automatons, speaking senseless drivel, controlled only by the sun's rise and descent. A 24 hour life span of time - numb from the neck up.

However, a good joint made life easier to understand. Luckily, there was plenty of weed available. We learned the secret of soaking the pot in opium before stuffing it into an emptied Kent cigarette. Four of us would fire one up, pass it around and stare at a burning candle for hours while saying nothing to each other except "Wow" or "Yea."

One such night, about 3:00 am, our perimeter got hit hard. The claymores were going off as the night lights from our 4-duce mortars lit the sky, but I could not find my M-16 to save my soul, I was so high. And that night marked the end of my smoking dope.

Some days ended with not caring about anything, some with fear of the next day, some with thoughts of home, some with thoughts of getting laid, some with exhaustion, and others without thoughts of any kind - and those days were the best.

Circumstances have a way of governing our lives, creating demands on how we live, and giving us purpose or reasons to get out of bed every day. Sometimes, if we're lucky, we get to choose - sometimes not. The powers of choice in Nam yielded to what was needed - and what was needed changed like the colors of a chameleon adapting to whatever it happens to be sitting on at the moment.

Such was the case with me as I found myself carrying a radio on my back - wondering how or why it ended up with me. I received no training for using one, yet suddenly there I was, folding my antenna down over my shoulder and tucking it into my ruck sack so Charlie wouldn't shoot me. It was their practice to shoot the guy with the radio first (for obvious reasons).

We have tendencies to excel at what we like - and for some unknown reason, I liked talking to chopper pilots, four duce mortar guys, artillery batteries and officers of all rank - and sometimes, Air Force fighter pilots.

Rank carried no weight on a radio, knowledge and keeping cool under pressure was the only criteria. There are no stripes or stars on a voice, but great respect was given to whoever could maintain their cool during intense situations - as I was to find out. I learned how to respond rather than react. When we re-act, we simply do what we did before - and in Nam, it was always different (which demanded the correct response from an RTO). Kinda' like playing billiards - because one never gets to shoot the same shot twice, as long as you play.

I got a crash course on map reading and protocol. I was on my way to OZ, but there was no yellow brick road leading me. I had no clue of how or why it happened, what was coming next or what to do the next day. It was another wave experience – I was out of control and reeling again. But hey, no more walking point or crawling in tunnels. This new assignment didn't hurt my feelings one bit. I gladly took the job.

As usual, surprises abounded and the common denominator in every lesson I learned was that meaningful knowledge came by way of "initiation by fire."

In order to guard our transmissions from being intercepted, our radios were fitted with what we called a "Ham on Rye." It was a wallet-sized, two piece gizmo with letters across the top and numbers down the side. Every day we would move to a new letter and a new number, then fold it together like a sandwich and slide it into the top of the radio. Only RTO's had them and we guarded the month's numbers and letters with our life - keeping them in weather proof bags. Our radios were PRC- 25's, so naturally they were called PRICK-25's.

I had to memorize frequencies for weather, artillery, mortars, air-force, ground pounders and the Tactical Operation Center (TOC) for our battalion - all of which would change periodically.

The serendipitous surprise for me was my newfound responsibility for someone other than myself. The accuracy of my communication skills overshadowed the accuracy of my shooting an M-16. This revealed a side of me I had not yet seen.

If the pen is mightier than the sword, my voice was more powerful than a machine gun – literally! I witnessed this as my adjusting calls to the 105 Howitzers moved the impacts closer and closer until they were going down Charlie's throat (with great pleasure, I might add).

It is amazing to me how life-changing pivotal events enter our time on earth, but are masked in insignificance. A little random gesture or a simple act of kindness viewed by a 5 year old boy will lodge in his memory bank, ushering him into the ministry in his adult life. Sometimes these pivotal events make profound impacts on us without our recollection of the event. Such was the case with a powder blue and white bumper sticker sent to me by my cousin Patsy. It simply read "THINK SNOW" in bold white letters.

I put it on the stock of my M-16, bought a box of popcorn, and watched the show. Everyone smiled, some laughed out of control and many made comments about shoveling the white stuff, skiing on it, making snow balls, or enjoying toboggan rides. Others recalled ice fishing, scraping windshields in the morning, snow plows smashing parked cars, icicles hanging from gutters, and making angels after a fresh snow fall in the front yard. And of course, we all laughed about warnings to never eat the yellow snow. For those of you who don't get that, ask a Yankee.

More importantly, those two seemingly insignificant words cut into the dominion of the three words that ruled my life up to that moment in time. "Don't mean nothin'" no longer meant nothin' – it didn't mean "0" either – it took on a different meaning; because nothing meant everything because everything ended in Vietnam. In Nam, you couldn't be the person you were at home. As a grunt, in order to live, you had to die. So, "don't mean nothin'" was the cost of admission into the world of non-feeling and not caring.

Sympathy was a word found in the dictionary in between sap and syphilis, but never seen in Vietnam. At any rate, some type of healthy seed got into the soil of my dead, "don't mean nothin'" existence without my notice when I glued those words to my M-16. Heaven only knows how many ears of corn will sprout off the stalk that started with that one kernel; leaving me today with the hope that my cousin's "THINK SNOW seed" found its way into the hearts of those who grinned when they looked at it.

How could my cousin know what she did? How can we know what happens when we opt to act on impulse? It wasn't just a bumper sticker, it was my ticket to come back to the U.S.A. and a life of freedom. Gotcha thinking, huh? Well, let me tell you how "THINK SNOW" changed my life in the next chapter.

Chapter 6
Captain Napoleon

The captain of our company was going home and we all were glad for him, but we were concerned about his replacement. It was a crap shoot. The rotation of replacement officers was like a sick game of Russian roulette - in that it never took too long before we knew if we got a winner or a dickhead.

Our new leader, Captain B, turned out to be a short, skinny guy - and short guys usually felt duty bound to prove themselves (which I'm sure is a trait studied in psychology 101). I believe they call it a "Napoleon complex."

He was also a screamer (which was a frowned upon characteristic that was most usually abandoned in a short time), but this guy was stubborn. He wasn't listening to his E-7's and E-8's - which was a very bad sign. He insisted on not waiting to be assigned a mission from Battalion Headquarters, but would volunteer his war-weary company at meetings in the TOC in order to show off and brown nose the Generals. On the other hand, he was a kick ass leader during a firefight and was not afraid to use his AR-15 (along with his screaming), so we decided the yelling and screaming could stay - for this guy only!

The abundance of his volunteering was another story, which would require time to fix, but time was a commodity valued above all others in Vietnam.

Value is determined by what someone is willing to exchange for what you have. This captain was under the impression he could exchange our lives in order to bolster his low self-esteem or advance his career by getting promoted to Major. He did this callously without considering the value of our lives. His ignorance of how to command in the field was about to put him in a plastic bag. The how's and why's were being discussed in small groups. It was an avalanche that could not be stopped once initiated. The fate of many officers in Nam was determined by the men they commanded, not the North Vietnamese.

The unique part about this guy was that he was liked by many of us, so it would take a clincher, some really dumb move on his part to turn the tide of the guys on the fence.

It didn't take long. We had just gotten back from a 4 day hump - up and down mountains in the rain, fighting leeches, snakes, and mosquitoes. Most of us had serious foot problems and we had not slept in days, but our illustrious captain volunteered us to help a surrounded platoon nearby. There was no moon on the night we walked out of our perimeter and they would not give us any night lights from our 4-deuce mortars. We couldn't see our noses in front of our face and we were expected to travel through dense jungle, without making any noise, to help a platoon that had probably been overrun by now since the shooting had ceased hours ago.

If anything, we were about to walk into a night ambush and we all knew it except for our Audie Murphy, John Wayne captain. Finally after several hours of this insanity, he decided to abort the mission and return to camp. This was the clincher for the guys on the fence. It now became unanimous. The questions that remained were, when, where and how - and of course, there was the "who." All of which would be answered quickly now!

Killing could be handled, managed or dealt with in battle, but cold blooded murder played havoc with my conscience. I pondered the difference without being able to justify either at times.

Trying to describe what happens when you take a person's life is like trying to put into words what you feel inside when you experience sexual intercourse with a woman you desperately love. Maybe it's because ending a life or creating one are both sacred things, momentarily released to a lessor realm of creatures - mere mortals, such as we all are.

In any case, something deep inside was telling me this was wrong. My options were few, but my decision about the captain proved to be one that would alter the course of my entire life.

We all deal with the "if only's" and the "what if's" as we ponder our past, but memories are more important than possessions. In many respects what happened as a result of this particular choice positively affected people around me in many ways - then and now. As another result, I've learned to not pay a whole lot of mental attention to my choices that turned sour.

I was about to break a rule - an unwritten rule. A rule I had never seen broken before. A rule that could get me killed or put me in prison for life – or sent home in a bag. So why not simply let things happen? Why jeopardize myself? I had witnessed what was going to happen many times, in many ways, never once questioning the madness. At some unknown point in time, my personal role in these affairs transitioned from that of an observer to that of an executor. Involuntary metamorphic changes had a way of justifying what was once cruel, obscene behavior into normalcy.

I glanced at the stock of my M-16, remembering the night my dad had to leave his 56' Plymouth hopelessly stuck in a mountain of snow several blocks away from our home. It was 9:30 at night and Mom was worried. Buffalo got hit with a major blizzard. Dad walked home to get his set of full chains for the rear wheels and asked me to walk back with him to help out. It was below zero that night, but the snow had ended. We stopped to buy a couple of Mars candy bars (with the almonds on top) on our way to the car because Dad missed dinner. It was the best tasting candy bar I had ever eaten from that day until now. Our fingers and toes got numb, our ears and noses turned red, but we returned home with that two-toned pink and white two door Plymouth. We bonded that night. Whatever needed fixing between us – got fixed that night. My very life changed that night - not just with my Dad, but with myself. I felt good about myself. I felt good about everybody after that night. I allowed that feeling to slip out of me and right then. I wanted those feelings back as I looked at those words "THINK SNOW" on the stock of my rifle.

"The nature of all men is so formed that they see and discriminate in the affairs of others, much better than in their own." Terence - 185-159 B.C.

It took many years to discover the answers to my questions about these matters, but with the answers came the peace that I still possess today. In a weird, upside down way of thinking, we are the authors of decisions, not the owners of results. So, come what may, I decided to crawl into the captain's hooch one rainy night, unannounced and uninvited, and tell him that he was about to die very soon because he was commanding like an asshole. Hey, when you're in water over your head, it doesn't really matter how deep it is!

Words cannot describe his reaction. He was instantly aware of the fact that my life would end if anyone found out that I had warned him. His initial reaction shocked me, but made me feel like I had made the right decision at the same time. He also knew that this kind of thing happened regularly, but never suspected it would happen to him. He was scared shitless and he was shocked at the news.

Having been in country for almost a year, put me in an unusual position. The guys respected me and most of the officers listened to me. Rank meant nothing as I've said before, but this incident proved it.

The words started to roll out of me. I hadn't planned what I said to him that night. It came out of me like vomit that I couldn't control or stop from erupting from deep within me. I told him to call a meeting first thing in the morning with all his Lt.'s and E-6's, E-7's and one E-8. I urged him to tell them that he was going to see the battalion commander "today" and that he'd get back to them with another meeting in the evening. Also, I told him to get hot chow sent in tomorrow and a double ration of beer for everyone.

I told him to act quickly. First thing in the morning, because the time may have already been set, so he had to move at the crack of dawn.

Then I told him to tell the battalion commander that his company desperately needed time back in base camp for showers, steam baths, women, beer, haircuts, hot food and time to write home, etc. Then he was to get back with the men tomorrow night and tell them what was going to happen. This had to go bing-bang-boom and he knew it!

After that, I told him to listen and take the advice of his sergeants who had been in country for a long time and especially to those who had previous tours under their belts.

He did it all like clockwork, just as I told him. We never talked about our conversation to anyone. In order to avoid suspicion, we purposely avoided each other from then on and had only occasional casual conversations.

His life was spared and mine took on new meaning.

Having to hold it back (what I had done) was no fun when all the guys were saying, "What the fuck happened to the old man?" "The old man's a good dude." And so on!

It was a carefully guarded secret that the captain and I kept between us. It was a secret worthy of an Academy Award as we acted out our joyful responses to the welcomed change.

Then suddenly, out of nowhere, came orders for me to be taken out of my line company and transported to Headquarters Company where I would be an official RTO instead of a fill-in operator when I was needed in the boonies.

After I got the news and told everyone (which was the cause of much beer drinking of course), the captain passed by and gave me a wink - like Santa Claus before he goes up the chimney. He said not one word and carefully timed his gesture so that only I could see him.

His wink spoke volumes and launched my life into yet another unknown world of new friends, new responsibilities, and an M-16 that spent more time slung over my back than being fired.

I changed how I used to think about short guys for the rest of my life and began to actually look forward to the tomorrows instead of dreading them.

It's incredible how our decisions determine our destiny - or should I say, responsibilities to ourselves! He thought my "THINK SNOW" bumper sticker was hilarious.

Chapter 7
Lucy

Adapting to an environment or a culture is a gradual process that all of us endure during our lives. This exercise is played out as we move from childhood to adolescence. Then adulthood moves in regardless of wherever we happen to be born - and the seasons change and vary excepting, of course, if we decide to move from Florida to Alaska.

Our bodies then make the automatic necessary adjustments from dealing with humidity to dry cold. Our minds deal with the shift because it was our decision to do so - and of course the longer we stay in one place, the more difficult it becomes to adapt to a new place.

Such was the case for me as I discovered the impact of being a 26 year old journeyman sheet metal worker with a wife and child one minute - then suddenly out of nowhere, I'm being surrounded by 18 and 19 year old kids just getting out of high school with no identities who were transported to a sauna-bath nightmare in the middle of Vietnam.

None of this was my decision, so my mind, body and spirit left me feeling estranged and in wonder of an uncertain future in a new world where no one knew me or spoke my language. I felt like a dog chasing his tail or a drunk bouncing off walls. I was in the middle of a spinning, changing, maze.

The reaction to the huge age difference between myself and the other "drafties" was entertaining and painted a clear picture of how people are raised. This insight helped me immensely and enlightened me as to who to trust and who to ignore or avoid, but now it was unimaginable shifting from jungle fighting to street fighting, to fighting amongst ourselves, to carrying a radio without a break, without a signal, without a season change, without a warning and without training.

The wonderment left without conscious awareness just as it arrived, giving me back my bearings and an acute wakeup call that was much needed from the radical transitions I was going through.

In a hospital operating room, a bunch of strangers walk into a 65 degree ceramic tile and stainless steel theatre, put on the Pink Floyd CD, and proceed to cut out your cancer infected lung, stitch you up, and wheel you out of the room.

And that's just how I felt inside. I had some things in me that were fucked up, but now they were coming out and life was going to be totally different - without a past, giving me a new lease to go on in life.

There is no actual cognition of the process going on inside us as we become pin balls bouncing through life - hitting, things all around us and never knowing where we'll wind up.

But now I was beginning to see how the fouled up events of my past were becoming tools that I could use to carve out my new future rather than allowing them to be the anchors holding me in patterns of failure and disappointment. I was discovering myself - my real self.

As a journeyman sheet metal worker, I had to learn the three methods of development used to fabricate any and every object that's made out of a flat sheet of metal. They are called triangulation, radial line, and parallel line development.

Once these are committed to memory, you have the ability to create anything you can see - regardless of size. We were taught to never be intimidated by size. When you understand the laws of refrigeration, you can install or repair the air-conditioning in the Empire State building or the window unit in your bedroom - just bigger pipes.

The process of development must be in your mind from start to finish before you take the hammer out of the tool box. In Vietnam we didn't survive using learned behavior, you needed acute instincts and intuition; which to my surprise, were inside me before I was drafted.

So it was with this rationale that I reasoned with myself at 26 years of age. Naturally, I didn't know what would happen after I became the one who was releasing the pin balls, rather than being the ball that was tossed around, but my newfound sense of awareness left me with a heightened confidence in myself that penetrated its way into my bones. I now had a radio on my back and I was damn good with it, but nobody taught me how.

So a fresh set of characters walked onto the stage of my new "twilight zone" life and I was comforted in knowing that maybe I was not the producer of the chaos, but I was at least an associate director now. This afforded me a measure of control I didn't have when the lights dimmed before the big feature began on my arrival in Nam. I had zapped a few dinks with my M-16, but with a radio I was killing hundreds of them.

I have no idea what the Army's training was like in the '50's or '40's but the '60's was nothing short of a Chinese fire drill - serving no purpose other than introducing you to the worst food on the planet .

We were dying like flies in Vietnam - which resulted in a demand for officers and drafted grunts to be produced like engines on a Ford plant assembly line. Green, inexperienced, mass produced lambs flying off to the Far East slaughter house - returning in body bags – accomplishing nothing.

People who never fought in a war were assigned to teach us how to fight. What were they thinking?

In boot camp, we trained with M-14 rifles that were used in WWII. We carried M-16's in Nam. I think I saw one M-14 during my year in country (which was in the hands of a South Vietnamese soldier). The gun was bigger than he was!

Our training officers were 20 year old kids who were barely sobered up from prom night. The seasoned sergeants were about to retire after having served in Korea or Germany and were too old to go to Vietnam.

The only war which many were familiar with was the Civil War (which they were still fighting). Before being drafted, I hadn't left Buffalo, New York, so the North and South bullshit was totally new ground for me.

It's far too complicated or stupid to figure out, but my last name stared with a "K", so I found myself in the company of many guys whose last name started with "K" from everywhere in the U.S. - or I should say, mostly south of the Mason Dixon Line.

I was a gangster because I was from New York. According to one of my E-7's from Alabama, I didn't even know what dirt was because all I lived in was concrete, glass, and steel.

Naïve as I was about the hatred that crept its way down through the generations, I jumped into the old battle (between the North and South, or between the Yankees and Confederates) as an amusement - only to find that some took it seriously; as if we didn't have enough to contend with already.

So war was on the agenda between Blacks and Whites, North and South - in boot camp, advanced infantry, and in the Republic of South Vietnam.

I reported to Fort Polk, Louisiana for 9 weeks of advanced Infantry Training in September of 1967. The climate and woods was as close to Nam as you could get back in the States. The training might as well have been done by aliens from Mars - except for a few guys who had finished their tour and were assigned as instructors to fill out the rest of their hitches.

One such bright and shining Lt. from the Carolinas was to be my company commander for AIT. He was fresh out of

O.C.S. (officer candidate school) and he was a Yankee hater to the core. The only thing we shared or agreed upon was our skin color.

He spoke of the Civil War and his disgust for Yankees every time he opened his mouth. We wondered if he was insane because he seemed so obsessed with the subject.

It was the practice of these mass produced "tin plated" officers to pick out one guy and hound him for all to see. It was a game to break someone down into losing his temper and swearing or taking a swing at an officer. The idea being to demonstrate respect to officers no matter what they say or do on the battlefield.

All the players in the game knew the score, but this particular Lt. was using the stage to vent a genuine hatred for Yankees – which, no doubt, was taught to him at the dinner tables and schools of his short life in Dixie.

I was to be the lucky recipient of his disdain for the northern part of the U.S.A. I was 26 years old, so I became "Gramps." And since I was from Buffalo, New York, I was the perfect candidate to scream at every day. From morning until night, he hounded me and no one else for nine weeks.

I developed some problems with my right knee about two weeks before the end of training. We ran everywhere all the time. Running was the common thread in the training that was used in all service branches in all the wars we ever fought.

But running became a major problem for me - and if I couldn't keep up with the guys, I would have to re-cycle the whole 9 weeks after spending some time in therapy.

The Lt. spotted my dilemma and turned up the pressure (especially while we were running). I would be the last guy in the ranks - usually trying to keep up while dealing with my bad knee. The pain would bring tears to my eyes. The Lt. would run backwards just in front of me calling me Gramps and asking about my arthritis, telling me to go back home to New York with all the rest of the fucking Yankees and on and on and on.

Quite to my amazement, I made it through the 9 weeks without punching the Lt.'s lights out. I wound up with one very sore knee and a distinct dislike for southern officers. No, let me change that to hatred. He did accomplish one thing in me however - which was to push me to hate enough where I could kill. About a year had passed, finding me working in a firebase near Dak To. I was told to go out to the L.Z. (landing zone) to greet some N.F.G.'S (New Fucking Guys). I was an RTO (Radio Telephone Operator) now - working in a T.O.C. (Tactical Operations Center). I was recommended for this position by my captain in the boonies who developed that funny habit of winking at me whenever our paths would cross - he was a Yankee, incidentally.

I had a good deal of jungle rot on the left side of my face, which prevented me from shaving on that side. After almost a year in the jungle, the red dirt had worked its way into the pores of my scalp and skin. The cuts and scrapes on my face and arms were surrounded with redness because we couldn't wash up or keep clean for any length of time.

I was a wreck. I had lost about 25 lbs. so the bones were showing in the wrong places and then I broke out with a case of pin warts on my neck. I had forty five of them under my chin. A med-a-vac surgeon took them off with a scalpel after hitting each one with a needle. Needless to say, I looked rough, but I wore a smile from ear to ear which kept everyone guessing except my favorite rebel Lt. (who lo and behold was the first guy I extended my hand to getting off the chopper at the L.Z.)

His eyes were as big as cue balls when he recognized me. It was his first day in country. There he was with his starched and pressed fatigues, fresh haircut, clean shaven face, and white as a ghost complexion. He was scared shitless with just a little bit of his girlfriend's good bye lipstick still on his cheek.

He actually greeted me with a big smile - I guess because he had finally seen a familiar face, but then he suddenly remembered who I was. I could see the visible change of his countenance. He noticed my physical condition. Then he felt my grip squeeze his knuckles and I yanked him off the chopper. His back pack made him top heavy so he fell down, rolling over in the dust while the rap of the chopper blades were smothering out his memories of home.

He said, "You remember me, don't you?"

I extended my hand to help him get to his feet and I stared into his eyes without blinking. I conveyed the most menacing glare of disgust I could muster. He read me like a book as his fear took the last remaining color away from his already pale complexion.

"Of course I remember you. Welcome to NAM" I said.

He tried to talk as we walked up to the TOC. He started to ask about how it really was in Nam. He asked if I'd seen any of the guys from AIT, but then he realized I was not going to answer or respond to anything he had to say.

The nonverbal communication took over as I wiped the smile off my face and stared into his eyes once more, but this time introducing him to the hell he had just entered. I could see the fear delivering it's strangle hold on him like a python squeezes its prey a little tighter every time it exhales. I was enjoying every moment of it (as he could plainly see). During his three days of indoctrination at the firebase, we passed each other a few times, but I said not one word – I just gave him the stare reserved only for the intense moments right before you pull the trigger. In spite of how he treated me, I felt sorry for him in a strange way – because I knew what he was about to experience. He avoided eye contact with me and was sent out to a line company shortly thereafter.

So now let me tell you about Lucy. For some unknown reason, I opted to take my R & R (five days wherever you choose to go) in the 10th month of my 1 year tour of duty. Hawaii sounded great, so off I went in November of 1968 - to the island paradise of the world.

It was a wakeup call to the fact that the world had not changed, but rather I was the one who had morphed into someone else. I had seen too much, done too much, justified too much, so I didn't fit in anymore. I felt alone and awkward - not able to respond to simple gestures or even questions from waiters and airline attendants. I couldn't sleep in that fresh, clean bed in that beautiful hotel on Waikiki Beach with the sliding doors open and the gentle breeze tugging at the sheer curtains. I could hear the waves breaking on the beach and the people laughing from my 6th floor oceanfront paradise.

The next day I decided to drink a bottle of scotch while sitting on the carpet with my back against the wall. I used room service for food. I had not slept in a bed nor sat in a chair or crapped in a toilet for almost a year. Finally I got the courage to go out on the beach.

I watched little kids making sand castles, dropping their ice cream suckers as they melted before they could eat them - and none of it made sense.

I rented a new red Chevy convertible, but I could only look at it. I drove it back to the parking lot of my hotel and just simply stared at it while drinking one beer after another. Nothing was familiar or fun.

I walked down Kalakaua Boulevard and watched the women shop and the young couples eat and drink in the sidewalk cafes. My feet didn't seem to touch the ground as I was unable to relate to concrete – especially while trying to adapt to flip-flops. I didn't belong there. I didn't belong anywhere.

I wanted to go back to Nam and get out of there because nothing was connecting with me anymore. I was sure that everyone was looking at me; seeing what I had done in

Nam. I was going to get killed when I went back, so I thought - so why did I want to go back? I didn't want to think that thought, but I couldn't stop my mind's desire to return there. My friends were back there, my only friends, and many were dead. I needed to be dead too, then I could be with them.

I met a door gunner the next day and a Marine who was a great guy, but he just wanted to get into fights everywhere we went. He always won without my help, but I only had two days left in paradise and I was on the prowl for some fun - or something other than fighting and killing.

I decided that gin and tonic with a twist of lime in the company of civilians would be the answer to all my problems! I needed to be with normal people who would converse about something other than war and killing. A quick glance at my hands revealed some dried up blood way up under my nails. Surely everyone would notice it, so I bought a stiff nail brush and went to work on the outside of me, but the inside was showing through and I couldn't do anything about it.

The Lemon Tree Lounge jumped into view along with their sign welcoming service men. It was a small, cozy place and I was greeted like a homecoming party with all of my aunts, uncles and cousins. I was wearing new "civies" which I bought at Sears the day before. Nothing I bought matched or fit and the only thing that was obvious was the neon sign on my forehead which read "I'm on R & R from Vietnam."

An elderly couple who were sitting at the end of the bar introduced themselves to me. They owned a 65 foot yacht and they were on the world voyage of their dreams. Needless to say, I was totally unable to buy drinks or spend a dime in this place. The gin was doing what gin does - bringing me to a numbness that kills the pain of a toothache or heartache.

Then "she" walked in and sat at the bar next to us. Her name was Lucy and my two new friends knew her, so they were happy to introduce us. I would have rather met her before all the gin and tonics, but then I tapped into my motto "Don't mean nothin" - and lo and behold, it worked.

Everyone knew what was happening except me. They had watched many a soldier drown himself in booze while trying to forget for a few days.

I ate something in an attempt to sober up a little so I could find the nerve to ask Lucy out for dinner and/or whatever. I couldn't take my eyes off of her "non-Asian" face. She had light brown straight hair and a nice figure. She was about 5'2" and wore a really big smile to hide the sadness inside. She was a nurse at a large local hospital.

The drinks were flowing which made a path for the conversation to switch from seriousness to foolishness and then just plain old out of control laughter. We were just people trying to make lifelong friendships in the span of one afternoon. People holding on to life that was seeping through our fingers - life that was leaving before having a chance to live it. Life cut off from destinations and desires. Valuable lives being sacrificed without rhyme or reason, but in that afternoon, we were relishing every moment of what we had together. Nobody was going to be cheated that afternoon - not even the bartender. The war was the reason we met, but not the subject of our conversation.

We were beyond normal social behavior. We were living in an out of control world, so there was no need to be concerned about feelings or offending each other. We were being pushed by man's inhumanity to man. We tapped into each other's intimate affairs of life without reservation. It was a welcomed invasion of privacy.

Back in the world, it would take weeks of small talk to get to what you actually wanted to say, but we got right to it, knowing full well it was going to be all over in one brief encounter, one afternoon, and one opportunity to grab the brass ring. After a couple hours and a belly full of gin, I thought - what the hell... why not?

So I asked Lucy to dinner. She told me she was engaged to a captain in Vietnam and I said, "I don't care! I just want to eat dinner and talk to a beautiful American woman - nothing else."

She relented and said "Well, ok then."

I asked where her favorite and most expensive place was. She was happy to pick, so I said, "Get dressed up and I'll pick you up at 7:00 with my red Chevy convertible."

She smiled and confirmed the date with a wink and a "Great."

We took a detour before dinner and decided to "Carpe' Diem" - if only for a few hours. We drove around the island smelling the pineapples ripening in the night air. Then we feasted on the best prime rib that I'd ever eaten (still to this day) and drank top shelf everything. I put the top down and we drove into the 75 degree salt air again after we ate - not paying any attention to directions or caring where we were going. We shared our life history along with all the hopes, fears and regrets as we watched the sun creep up over the bluest Pacific Ocean in recorded history.

When we met I thought of how wonderful it would be to make love to such a gorgeous woman, but by the time we parted after walking up to her apartment to say goodnight, love making was the farthest thing on my mind. Thoughts of love making were replaced with a wish for her and her captain to live long and enjoy life to its fullest when he came back from Nam. I kept it to myself, but couldn't help thinking, "He won't come back alive."

I asked her for a good night kiss and I got one right away. We wrapped our arms around each other and held on for dear life. For those brief moments, I was her captain and she was my girlfriend back home. We kissed this way and then that way and we both knew it was time to say goodnight.

I asked her for another date tomorrow night and she said, "I would love to, but after that kiss I don't think we should."

I reluctantly agreed. So I never saw her again - except in my dreams.

When two people think and say the same thing at the same time, it's customary to hook your little fingers and make a wish - which is exactly what we did on that unforgettable morning.

I've often wondered if Lucy's captain came back alive.

Chapter 8
Kaleidoscope Life

I couldn't wait to get back to Nam and my buddies. I wanted to fast-forward time, get it over with and behind me.

I stayed drunk for the remainder of my stay in Hawaii. I fell asleep on Waikiki Beach and got sun burned legs. I had a decent tan on my upper body from taking off my shirt in the jungle, but I never took off my pants, so my legs were white as ghosts.

Most all of us experience times of transition; which can have devastating effects if we find ourselves at a loss of awareness or in wonder of simply what the heck is happening. This R & R experience was one of them!

When the dentist pulls a tooth or two, you launch uncontrollable searches into the vacant spot, finding this volcano sized cavity that you're sure no one could possibly even imagine. After all, you're walking around in someone else's body and your mind can think of nothing besides that strange, empty cavity. Gradually you find the courage to reckon with the reality that you will never again be the same person because you now have this hole in your head and you have to move on. Transitions can be impossible at times - and that's where I was in 1968. Constant change was there to stay.

Cutting your fingers in a sheet metal shop, running up and down hills in Kentucky, shooting people and dogs and pigs, kissing beautiful women, flying in 707's - then more killing and more killing - all the while trying to find the tooth that used to be right there - or was it ever really there?

Like squeezing a tube of toothpaste, the pressures of life expose who we really are inside. No one likes pressure, so we avoid it - and consequently, we never find out about our inner man.

When you release a baby in a pool of water, they will swim - or at least keep their head up because they unconsciously remember life in the womb. It's not a decision, but a response.

We feel guilty about the bad or wrong decisions in our past, but never our responses (which we rightly defend even if they got us into trouble) because they were concocted in our sub-conscious mind.

What we do does not define who we are. There are innocent men and women behind bars who feel not one twinge of guilt as they live with the pain and agony of everyday life behind bars. Yet they are at peace with themselves inside because they know they're innocent victims.

I didn't discover until 40 years after Nam how internal thought governs external action - or ignores it, or is blind to it, or denies it, or doesn't consider it, or is surprised by it - and so on.

We're all schizophrenics in a way. We're on a stage acting out our performances in front of audiences who didn't pay to get in; while being amused by our portrayals of who we think we are - or dream of being down deep inside. Or maybe it's more like a sneak preview of yourself before the main attraction. In Vietnam, the option to see the main attraction didn't exist. It was just a matter of time before you found out what you're made of (a short amount of time if you were a grunt).

We touch each other for more reasons than we know. Like ants traveling in a frenzy, migrating back and forth from a discarded sucker on a sidewalk to their volcano mountain home, but always stopping to touch each other on the way. I wonder why they do that.

Something real and vitally important takes place in us and to us at every encounter. It's registered in our sub-conscious, without our awareness, when we stop to touch whoever shows up in our path. The world is a stage - make no mistake! I sat on that hard chair in my shrink's office 45 years later - listening and watching as he chipped away at the obstacles which stood in the way of me being who I really am and who I was destined to become.

Meaningless, insignificant events in my past became monumental benchmarks available to me when I needed them. Events in a battle field 40 some years ago became the deciding factors of decisions made in the NOW of my life. The curtains were being pulled back and I was beginning to see!

Each one of my visits to "the shrink" would turn things around for me to observe - revealing what was hidden or behind the doors I refused to open.

My shrink, Dr. N, would turn the tubes of my "kaleidoscope life" and shuffle all of the different shapes, sizes and colors around and around. Then it began to appear - a beautifully designed, perfectly proportioned picture, fitting together in a magnificent pattern, developing more and more with every little turn and twist. Then he would say "Well Ken, our hour is up."

But it was progress I hadn't seen in 4 decades. Finally, there was a light at the end of the tunnel.

He told me of two psychiatrists who had written extensively about the unusual number of suicides among WWII vets in the '60's and '70's. The pattern was very predictable. In 1945, all our troops came home, went to college, got married, had kids, worked 20 or so years, and then retired. While occupied with the challenges of life, their ugly memories laid dormant for the most part. When retirement time came, their old memory bank began to occupy the free time with the hurt, pain and anger of the unfinished business and unreconciled horrors of war. It was history repeating itself after Vietnam.

My wife passed in 2007 of a very rare disease called Wegener's Glandular Lomatosis. It strikes 1 in 100,000, so I was told. They treated her for everything except that disease. Two weeks before she died, they gave her one dose of chemotherapy. The chemicals exploded some tuberculosis in her right lung (which had been there for 40 some years and had caused no ill effects whatsoever).

They greeted me with the news and with smiles on their faces because finally they were able to handle what they knew was one of her problems – or so they thought. I'll spare you the details of her demise. I trust you get the analogy.

Such was the case with my unexpected mental struggles that erupted 40 years later after Vietnam. I was shadow boxing an invisible enemy who answered the bell round after round, but my psychologist friend was turning the tubes of my "kaleidoscope life" at every session. I wasn't looking through the cross hairs on my M-16, but rather at a collage of events that had been lying there dormant for over 40 years. Now these hidden demons were being uprooted and I was transitioning into a normal human being with a bright future - which I was starting to look forward to. So I pulled my shoulders back, lifted my head up, put a smile on my face and said "I'll see you in two weeks."

I asked him once "How long is this, ahh, going to ahh... you know?"

He calmly answered with reassurance "As long as it takes, Ken."

Thank God for the VA and all of the dedicated people who work there. Words cannot express my gratitude and how thankful I am for their professionalism and courtesy.

Back in Nam, the sum of all fears laid in the haunting, ever-present possibility of being captured. The stories of what happened in POW camps ushered in the thoughts and conversations of what the Japanese did to our captured soldiers in WWII. We were scared shitless of it happening to any one of us.

We didn't know any of the circumstances of how it came about, but one of our guys (an E-4) in my company was taken prisoner during a routine day while climbing a mountain near the Cambodian border.

Everyone was drilled about what to do if you got captured - and luckily, my un-named comrade was awake during that class.

He said it was like an auto accident. He didn't really know how or why it happened. Like shaking off the shock of impact, he shook his head from side to side in an attempt to get present in the moment of just what in the hell was going on. He was gagged immediately. They tied his hands behind his back, took off his boots and socks and they beat him badly. He was taken to their base camp which was only about 2 klicks from where he was captured. It was downhill most of the way. He remembered from training how to take note of the terrain and direction he was going as it would become the route of his return back to his company's location - if he could escape.

Luckily, it only took a couple of hours to get to their camp. They locked him up in a crudely constructed bamboo box that was lashed together with vines. It was so small that he had to be stuffed in - and once inside, he was unable to move a muscle.

As the sun set on his first and only night of captivity, he pulled and twisted his way out of the thin ropes that bound his hands - cutting up his wrists in the process. Then he patiently waited until everyone was sleeping before he attempted to struggle his way out of the door of the small bamboo box.

As luck would have it, the two NVA soldiers guarding him got drunk in celebration of the prize they would get for capturing one of us. He pushed and shoved all night long. He managed to conjure up some energy from what little food and water was still in his body from the day before. Staying hydrated was the most important point they taught in survival class. It's easy to dehydrate quickly in the jungle and the NVA will starve you, so strength leaves your body rapidly. He broke out of his cage shortly before dawn and escaped the camp unnoticed.

Our E-4 knew it was necessary to move quickly because the morning light would bring patrols out to re-capture him. His feet were being steadily chewed up by the sharp grass and roots of the trees and his wrists were bleeding from the ropes he wriggled out of. His strength was leaking out of him in the form of his blood (which also provided a trail for the NVA to trace his escape route).

Luck came to him again in the form of a drenching rain which washed away his trail of blood. He used vines as tourniquets to slow down the bleeding from his hands and feet.

Two days and one night later he came limping up to our perimeter. Our reactions were a sight to behold – there was laughter, tears, and awe in the faces of the two guys who had just arrived in the field for their first day in the boonies as they watched him limping and staggering up to our perimeter.

Then and now, witnessing events like these usher us all to the thresholds of decision – whether they happened 40 years ago or yesterday is irrelevant.

Do we put down our heads and follow the crowd? Do we allow ourselves to melt in and settle for the status quo? Or do we opt to risk being different and challenge the forces that drive us? Tough questions, but the heroism seen in the movies back home was looking like gross stupidity in Vietnam because there were valid alternatives to winning battles which didn't require loss of life. Death was a part of life in Nam, but senseless sacrifice of precious life was hard to swallow and invoked the rebellion that was spoken of many years later in the documentaries.

The Army teaches safety in numbers, but living by the book crushes individualism and allows no place for uniqueness or free thought.

Comparison is not only the thief of joy, but it stifles the deep desire inside us to vocalize what we really feel, do what we really want, or just stand up in the classroom of a seated humanity.

In hindsight (which is always 20/20), I could plainly see how the impact of my radical decisions pulled me away from the crowd of the norm. Diverging from this insanity saved my life. We've all heard statements from returning soldiers like, "I have no idea why I did all that terrible shit" or, "Yeah, I just did what I had to do." This makes me sick because it's simply not true. No matter what we must face in life, we can still choose. Young or old, smart or stupid - WE are not robots. My true identity deep down inside me overcame the Army brainwashing. Forty years later, I could see, bigger than Dallas, how dangerous my decision was to tell my captain what was about to come down in his life. That single decision altered the course of my own life in a profound way - and nobody forced me to make it.

The most common regret that passes through the minds of people on their death beds is that they didn't take more risks. That adage does not apply to grunts who survived 1968 in Vietnam.

Ten months of walking point, being a tunnel rat, and surviving some 25 combat assaults (CA's) - along with my unexpected and serendipitous relationship with a radio, placed me at yet another door of one of those aforementioned thresholds of decision.

Chapter 9
Unforgettable Characters

This is my first attempt at writing anything – let alone a book. I attended an afternoon seminar at my local library entitled "Is There a Book in You?" It was very informative and inspiring, but the central piece of advice given by all four authors who spoke was to "just write, don't worry about what people will think." So let's credit them and continue.

Scrolling down the list of credits of my unforgettable characters and/or decisions in Nam brings me to the infamous Lt. T.

The Army assumed he was officer material - perhaps because of his college degree, but we all know the definition of the word assume.

He had a silver spoon in his mouth - which came from the set that his father had gotten his from and his father before him as well. One of his grandfathers evidently made a ton of money and passed it on down through the generations. Lucky him, unlucky me!

The Army was impressed with his genealogy and money, but I was not about to be made an ass of or die as a result of the Army's blindness.

He was an overweight, dumpy-shaped guy - which was another of his inherited conditions seen in the family photos (along with his freckles).

His milk toast complexion and profuse sweating evidenced the fact that he had just arrived in country.

It takes a few weeks to adjust to Vietnam's extreme climate. At first, you sweat a great deal because of the heat and humidity. Then as time goes on, you urinate less because your body is trying to retain water, so I was told.

Great machines these bodies of ours are with all of their built in mechanisms for survival. Which is more than I can say for the Army's decision making process in its assumption that T was officer material!

In a way, I felt pity for him like you would for that un-athletic kid who was always picked last for team sports in grade school gym class. The T's were always the last guys to be chosen. But Vietnam was not a sandlot baseball game, and this ding dong's silver spoon was of the sterling variety.

My momentary feelings of sadness and pity for him quickly disappeared when I was assigned to be his R.T.O. on a very unusual mission. I was going to have to take orders from this green Lt. who knew nothing about Vietnam. It was going to be just the two of us. Our company commander figured he would send me (a guy with 10 months in country) with the green Lt. so I could teach him the ropes; thus giving him the opportunity to benefit from my experience in the field. Well the captain failed to inform my Lt. of his intentions and left me with this piss pot who thought we were back in the states playing soldiers.

I knew how to handle new Lt.'s back in my platoon with my buddies, but this was a different ballgame. When he demanded that I call him "Sir" I knew I was in deep shit. I had to handle this all alone, but I had learned the art of self-reliance and survival – which prepared me for the Lt's in my life.

I attended a briefing in the TOC where I was given the frequencies to be used and all the maps with grid points and pre-plots. We were going to work with some special forces in an "A-camp" near Duc Lap.

I was told to study and familiarize myself with the terrain all around the camp. The grid maps where highlighted with suspected sights of NVA and recent troop movements with trails used by the VC as well.

The pre-plots had been established by a battery of 105 Howitzers with the 173rd Airborne.

Pre-plots were numbered locations on a map that the 105's worked out with forward observers with pinpoint accuracy - enabling us to nail Charlie when the first round was called for, usually!

So the stage was set. I actually had no need for the Lt.; however, Army protocol called for an officer to be at the helm.

We were to report to the A-camp and assist them with our red-leg (artillery) battery however or whenever they needed us to support their patrols or the camp itself - if necessary.

I was trying to get rid of the jungle rot on my face (which looked horrible) along with the cuts and bug bites after 10 months in the boonies. My appearance was a bit scary. My helmet cover listed the hills I had survived and the campaigns I had endured to date. My M-16 was scratched up badly and showed the tell-tale signs of heavy usage. I still had my same rifle, boasting the bumper sticker that was sent to me by my cousin back in Buffalo which boldly stated, "THINK SNOW." Those words always produced a smile and a wake-up to discouraged grunts who were in need of such - except for my asshole Lt. who ordered me to scrape it off.

We jumped off the Huey on the A-camps LZ and were greeted warmly by a Sergeant E-5 who took one look at us and simply grinned. He grabbed my hand first. He looked straight into my eyes and told me everything I needed to know without one spoken word.

He said "hi" to the silver spoon without a hand shake followed by a head turn telling him to come up to the main bunker.

We crept down into a deep bunker and were greeted by a Captain who offered us a cold beer. We sat at a table with 2 E-7's and an E-8. After a glance at my helmet cover, our conversation gravitated around (and/or about) what I had experienced in the past 10 months. My Lt. was steaming with anger.

It turned out the A-camp was relatively new and most of the members of the team had only been in country for a few weeks. They heard stories about the campaigns I had been in and were told by their instructors everything concerning these battles I had survived. So when they got to meet someone who had actually been there, they were all ears because they wanted to know what really took place.

My Lt. looked like a 10 year old kid who was waiting to be chosen to play right field as he was taking all this in. He was really pissed at all the attention I was getting and he ordered me out of the bunker (much to the dismay of the green berets).

I was so sick of all this bullshit. I had to fight off the growing desire to just be home - back in good old Buffalo, NY (which was now 60 days away). So I just grabbed a six-pack of Budweiser, took a short walk around our perimeter, and decided to sit on a bunker, get a little drunk and enjoy a quiet afternoon while surveying the surroundings of my new temporary home.

Experience has no substitute! 45 years after Nam, I'm sitting with my friends at Starbucks listening to questions they asked of me about battles I fought in back in Nam. They were just like the questions asked by those Special Forces guys who were trained well, but wondered, as all men do, about how they would hold up under fire - and of course, there was the big, impossible to answer question of "what is it like to kill someone?"

Now and then in life we collide with a wanna–be, like my Lt. who floats through existence - seemingly above it all in a "never-never land" occupied only by himself and his own selfish self-interests. Talking to him was like speaking to someone who was paying no attention to a word you're saying. If you tell them that you raped their mother and then cut her arms and legs off, they would respond, "Oh! That's great! Well I have to get going, so I'll see you soon. Okay, Ken?" Well that was my Lt. - need I say more?

What I failed to mention about this A-camp was that I thought I was in a 5-Star Hotel. We had a momma-san cook who made fresh donuts every morning. She even had medically checked out prostitutes for us. Hot food and all the cold beer you wanted - and nothing to do except play poker and write letters to send home. This was not the Nam I knew, but I was beginning to like it - until the sun went down. We spent our first hot, lazy afternoon firing rockets. They came in a four-pack and were mounted on the sides of a Huey. I have no idea how they got there or why we needed them. It just seemed like a fun thing to do, so we set them up on sandbags, hooked wires from claymore charging devices to the tails and fired them west into Cambodia while we drank a bunch of beer. Did I mention there was always lots of beer at this A-camp?

The top of our hill was only about 300 feet in diameter, but it housed a deep bunker that was covered with thousands of sand bags at the peak. Down off the crest about 20 feet was triple concertina razor wire surrounding the entire hill. Then 30 feet down from that wire was a row of apron wire with more concertina inside the triangular shaped maze of razor blades. The apron was 5 feet high in the center and 10 feet wide with woven strands going from bottom to top weaving into each other and forming a network of openings no larger than a lunch box at any given point.

We also had 100 or so C.I.D.G's (or mercenaries as they were sometimes called) surrounding the knob on top. I had heard about MIKE Forces which was the acronym given to these mercenary type warriors. They were ferocious fighters, but I never actually worked alongside them before.

The first evening was uneventful except for a winning night of 5-card stud - and a detailed play by play of hill 684 on Chu Moor Mountain in Kontum Province (which they had all heard about).

In the morning, claymores were being set up all around the perimeter and we were stocking the six fighting apertures around the peak with lots of ammo.

We didn't have to be told what was about to happen. We had M-60 machine guns in each bunker and a 50 cal. machine gun with its tri-pod anchored into a 55 gallon drum filled with cement.

The adrenalin was beginning to flow as the sun was slipping into the horizon - this was promising to be a very different experience from what I was used to. It was like I was driving to work in a different car every day. Nothing was ever the same. There was no repetition. The only constant event was death.

The night held no promise of a bright moon (which afforded Charlie the element of surprise). It wasn't that I hadn't been here before - then it hit me - I was in the company of guys who had never been in a real firefight. That's what was different - that's why I felt strange. Except for a few, I couldn't count on these guys (especially my silver spooned wonder boy).

"War makes strange bedfellows." Shakespeare was right!

This was like starting all over again from the beginning. It was a thought which brought me no comfort. Then I recalled the day when I heard that voice and realized it was emanating from deep within me: "I'm not going to die here. I'm going to make it out of here." There it was - I could hear it again, and I was much comforted.

So I pushed the re-wind button in my head and fell fast asleep. We set up our claymores in between the double apron and the triple concertina wire along with trip wires that would set off little flares that would warn us of where Charlie broke through.

The VC cut a hole in the apron wire and were coming close to the concertina when they started tripping off the flares.

We popped our claymores and the fun began. We had a 4-deuce mortar on the hill, so we sent up some night lights which illuminated the sky like a Friday night high school football game in a small stadium back home.

Half of the VC were trying to climb up our hill while the other half were retreating. They were all hip deep in wire.

It was like shooting ducks in a gallery. I didn't use my old faithful M-16 because I didn't want to seize it up from rapidly firing one clip after another. The machine guns were dropping them like flies - and as they fell and rolled down the hill, we just kept pumping more rounds into their already dead bodies.

When the 50 cal hit them, arms and legs were torn from their bodies, but they kept coming. It was unbelievable! They must have been doped up or something because they just keep coming. We were amazed beyond belief.

I burned up two M-16s and was working on my third when we heard a retreat whistle. The NVA liked whistles for some reason - and so did we, especially when they sounded this one.

The MIKE force lost a few people, but we only suffered two minor injuries - and a major mess in the morning.

The body count was in the hundreds, so they sent us a dozer to bury the bodies. We covered them with lime and shoved them in a huge pit. I was one day closer to a Buffalo, New York winter.

Chapter 10
That's All I'm Gonna Say About That

I have no degree in psychology from Harvard or Yale, but I'm pouring my heart and soul into these pages. My repeated attempts to explain myself or understand what was going through my mind 40 plus years ago resides at the very core of this effort. This is my attempt to reveal, to expose, to explain, to explore, and to immerse you into me and try to share what goes on in the mind when you kill a human being or watch one die in the field of battle.

Hopefully this writing will find itself in the hands of someone who is preparing to venture into harm's way, somewhere in this world, in defense of our country.

There is no doubt that we are all unique, one-of-a-kind creatures, so we see things differently. Nevertheless, it's my wish for this to be a note in a bottle that washed up on a beach to be found by the one person who needs it most.

"Killing" is a word that has many definitions and variations. There are many types of killing and reasons to kill. There is Jihad killing, executions for crimes, ethnic cleansing - like the WW-2 concentration death camp killing of the Jews. Killing can be an act of passion, an act of love and caring - like putting down a sick dog or a horse with a broken leg. There's killing for money in an armed robbery - or as a sacrifice to God, or in the Coliseums of Rome for amusement, and for righteous causes in a war. Some kill out of anger – and some kill because everyone else is. There is also self-defense - kill or be killed. I'm sure you can think of other reasons.

The day my wife died, the minister in the hospital gave me a small, but most informative book about grief. I stuffed it in my back pocket and forgot about it as I left the hospital that day.

Death is an enemy regardless of what form it enters our lives; whether it be a battle field or an operating room. We will all experience the effects of death - much the same as we handle the grief that inevitably follows. I did not shed a tear when my father died - and we were very close. It was the same when my mother died - not a tear. My wife called me a cold fish. I loved my mom and dad, but I couldn't cry. Thirty three years had passed since my tour in Nam, but its hold on me was firm. When my wife passed in 07', I cried for a few minutes the morning after she died and, to this day, that was it.

Vietnam is not like Las Vegas - because what happens there goes home with you.

Reading about the stages of grief in my little pamphlet paralleled my deepest feelings about the killing in Vietnam.

Death is death - whether you're responsible for it, or just a bystander watching a spreading pool of blood surround the head of a kid who just hit a tree with his motorcycle.

Grief is grief - whether you're counting the bullet holes in the chest of the gook you just shot or holding the hand of your grandmother as she takes her last breath.

131

We're not dogs who sniff the dead carcass of an old buddy with an expressionless scowl and then turn to their master and wag their tail because they see a Frisbee and want to play. No, no - we are complex creatures acting in response to the contents of our deep subconscious. The animal kingdom has one up on us all in respect to death and grief, I guess!

In all my combat training, they didn't tell us that you will most assuredly be a different person after you take the life of another human being.

After studying my little book on grief, I knew what to expect and was able to prepare myself.

Knowledge is power - and I received that power to walk away. I said good bye to my wife - and hello to the rest of my life.

The business of killing and dealing with death could be handled intelligently if addressed properly - just like my little mini book about grief, but somebody had to put it in my hand when I needed it.

I for one, am convinced that if our military would indoctrinate and thoroughly teach our men and women about the subjects of killing, death, and grief, we would not have all the PTSD (Post Traumatic Stress Disorder) problems in the lives of our returning veterans.

I was one very confused and troubled man inside when I came home from Nam - and I didn't even know it. However, lack of knowledge does not stop the effects any more than ignorance of the law will not excuse you from doing 45 in a

30 mile an hour zone. If you know the cause, you can work on the effects and stop them, numb them, tolerate them in some way, or at least deal with them. Ignorance of the mental problem does not make it go away.

Remember the commercial with the service station mechanic who said, "Pay me now or pay me later." He meant get an oil change now or a valve job later. Can we not see the forest for the trees here? Is this too simple?

Well, as Forest Gump said, "And that's all I'm gonna say 'bout that."

Let's get back to my silver spooned wonder boy Lt. Two of the Special Forces guys in the A-camp were seasoned veterans who had previous tours under their belts. All the rest were green along with my Lt.

The clean-up and repair to the wire took a few days, so me and the two green berets shared our previous battle stories and experiences with the others.

I watched my Lt. when we talked and noticed how our words flew over his head like a home run going over the fence in center field.

Earlier I shared with you how most of our K.I.A.'s (Killed In Action) got hit in the first 45 or the last 45 days of a one year tour. This was very accurate information and we were taught extensively about why this was so.

For the sake of a nutshell re-cap; the first 45 days you're green, the last 45 days you become over-confident and get sloppy.

The three of us observed as some of the guys were paying close attention while others were falling victim to the second most important piece of information you needed to stay alive in Nam - which was... well, let me say it this way. One of the most dangerous and costly things that can happen in Vegas is for you to win the first time you gamble.

The same was true in Vietnam. Never underestimate your enemy! We tried to tell them that what had just happened was a once in a lifetime event and not the norm. We warned them not to be deceived - just like they tell you in the reading material on the front desk at the Bellagio. It's amazing, they tell everyone what their odds are - they don't hide it from you or try to deceive you, and neither were we.

You cannot underestimate Charlie - and if you do, you will die. You cannot play blackjack too long because if you do, you will lose your money, DUH! You might catch Charlie with his pants down, but it's a rare occurrence. You might get a hot streak playing black jack, but if you keep playing, you will lose your house back home, your wife, your job and your fucking life.

In my last week of training at Fort Polk, Louisiana, we attended a late afternoon class on claymore anti-personnel mines. They were to be as much of a part of our lives as food. Every night we would set up the mines some 50 feet in front of our bunkers along with trip flares. They saved countless lives and there was a precise science as to how to set them up (as we were to find out).

Our instructor was a 19 year old, short skinny, white guy who was mild mannered and soft spoken. We had already gone through a full day of heavy physical training and it was a hot humid lazy Louisiana afternoon. About half way through the class, some of us were falling asleep - including me.

Suddenly the kid went up about 4 octaves and told us, and I quote, "I don't give a flying fuck if you all die in Vietnam, and I guarantee, you will - if you do not know how to use this claymore."

He continued, "I did my time you assholes, and I ain't goin' back, but you will come back in a fucking bag if you do not know how to use this goddamn claymore - so wake the fuck up!"

Our eyes were like cue balls after that and I never forgot one word of the instruction he gave us. This kid knew his shit about claymores - more so than the Army manuals because he actually used them and learned the tricks. They don't teach the tricks in manuals, but you have got to know them if you expect to get back home. Sorry silly rabbit - tricks aren't for kids, they're for GRUNTS.

I remembered that young instructor and I tried to talk to these new guys, not the way he did to us in Fort Polk, but with the same heart. My Lt., however, was acting like a nine year old brat who missed his nap on his first trip to the Magic Kingdom at Disney World.

I decided to save my breath and just watch my Lt. like a spider watching a fly - or like the cameras on the crap tables in the Aria or the Golden Nugget; watching good people throw their lives down the toilet.

During the course of our lives we find ourselves dovetailed with all kinds of people. People who occupy the desk next to yours - or, as in my case, the 15 guys who were sent by the union hall to install air-conditioning duct work in an office building. We would see each other every day for 40 hours a week for the next 6 months. Some were nice guys and others were jerks. Some ended up becoming good friends and others you didn't even bother to say good morning to because they were such assholes.

The definition of the word relationship took on a whole new meaning in Vietnam. I found myself yoked with a person who would get me killed, sure as God made green apples. This was no back home office building experience for me with this mamma's boy Lt.

I didn't like it, but I was in the kill or be killed slot and I was all alone on this one. He was the officer, I was the R.T.O. and the clock was ticking louder and quicker by the minute.

Up to this point there was no need for artillery, so we were just tagging along in the wings waiting to be called on stage.

The hot food was great, there was plenty of beer, and I was winning at poker (which was one of the many lessons learned from my dad). It pays to listen to your Dad - money won is sweeter than money earned, so they say. Ah, did I mention the abundance of beer?

Our little R & R was about to end. We attended a briefing about what we were doing and where we were going the next day. A large number of NVA troops were spotted on a re-supply mission headed toward one of their major base camps.

The silver spoon Lt. and I were to take 75 CIDG's and two Special Forces sergeants and essentially cut off their mission. As I previously stated, I had not worked with a MIKE force - so it was, for me, another new event which compounded my fears. I sent a coded message to the Artillery battery with grids and ETA's and we all proceeded down the yellow brick road with the MIKE force in the lead.

On the third day of our humping mountains, we were walking west on a ridge line. We were down from the top about 500 feet and we were right on the Cambodian border - or in Cambodia. It was difficult to tell.

The jungle was very dense and there was a thick canopy of vegetation above us which blocked out most of the daylight. Occasional small openings in the thickness would create flashlight-like shafts of light that would become spotlights that cut through the haze of steaming clouds of mist that would gracefully move about as the gentle breezes would push them to and fro. It was an eerie, tense atmosphere.

Without saying a word to each other, my eyes met those of the two Green Beret Sergeants. There was an unmistakable glare of horror. The silence was deafening. Suddenly, there was no monkey chatter, no birds were squawking. The air was so thick that breathing out was easier than breathing in. We turned our heads towards the top of the ridge. I swallowed the lump in my throat and clicked my M-16 to auto.

The Lt. was pissing and moaning about his sore feet. He was acting like a spoiled 5 year old sitting in a shopping cart at the check-out line screaming for a Milky Way bar that his mother refused to buy. He was un-fucking believable!

Like watching a king cobra with his head fanned out wide while docking and weaving as he surveys his prey, it was getting down to the seconds of what was inevitably going to be a quick strike attack. Charlie was about to open up on us any second. Only three of us could taste it - the rest were swatting bugs and bitching about the heat.

There was a micro-second between seeing the muzzle flashes and hearing the bullets whiz past your head. It looked like blinking Christmas lights on the eaves of a wide, ranch style house. The tracers were coming towards us at a rate I had never seen. There must have been hundreds of NVA shooting at us.

Every fifth round was a tracer - putting four rounds in between the lights that were taking on the appearance of the vortex you would see on the screen when Captain Kirk would ask Scotty for warp speed.

My next moves were instinctual. Without having to be told, the 75 CIDG's ran up the hill directly into the NVA while screaming and firing their 30 caliber carbines. It was a sight to behold for sure. We all followed them from behind. I made radio contact with the 105's telling them to get prepared. The bullets were popping on both sides of me as I eased up my pace and positioned myself directly behind the Lt. as we climbed the hill. It was like driving behind a tractor trailer on I-95 letting him catch all the bugs while you stay in his draft and enjoy the ride. I didn't plan it, it just happened - like another one of those little tricks not found in the training manual, this was learned by those who were smart enough to stay awake and pay attention in class and in combat.

My Lt. stopped an AK-47 round with his right leg. It gave him a trip home and an impressive 2nd page on his resume.

The MIKE force kicked the shit out of the NVA without anyone's help. They spoke a strange sounding language, but smiling is universal and they enjoyed shooting the dead bodies and encouraged us to join in the fun after the battle was won. My Lt. refused to join in, not having the stomach for it, until they stared at him with a kind of stoic glare that gave me a chill just watching. They didn't even care that he had been shot in the leg because shooting dead bodies was part and parcel of the victory - like eating the heart of that buffalo in the movie "Dances with Wolves" with Kevin Costner.

My friends and I made it through one more day in paradise. The brass was happy and the NVA's base camp was attacked and overtaken due to lack of ammo and food.

Everyone benefited that day except the poor woman who was destined to be the silver spoon's wife. So now, let's hear about - S!

S came into our lives at Headquarters Company and enjoyed a very brief stay. He was one of the most unforgettable characters I had the pleasure of meeting during my one year tour.

S was a sterling example of the U.S. Army's inability to place people where they could serve the best by utilizing their talents and gifts acquired - whether God-given or learned in civilian life.

To digress for a moment, but remain on topic, let's go back to my first three days in country. I arrived in Cam Ranh Bay via a Pan Am 707 in December of 1967. Before the war, it was the vacation destination of the rich jet setters of the world. Cam Rahn Bay made Miami Beach look like the Jersey Shore in winter time.

White sand beaches with crystal clear greenish-blue water allowed you to study the crabs and little bait fish on the bottom of the 8 foot deep water at the end of a dock just as clear as viewing the activity in your living room aquarium.

Little huts were built on poles in no particular order on the beaches - just high enough so the incoming tides would be just below the floor so as to not interrupt your honeymoon love making. What used to be very posh restaurants and hotels on the shore were now boarded up buildings waiting for this bullshit to end.

My eyes were feasting on all this opulence as I put my gear in the barracks. I was greeted by an elderly momma-san that walked crookedly as she swept and straightened up around my bunk.

All she could say was, "G.I. number one" and nothing else. Then she held out her hand for a tip. She smiled, showing me all her blackened teeth that were stained from chewing beetle nuts, when I gave her, in piaster, what would be 50 cents American.

We went to the air conditioned mess hall and feasted on some great food, then strolled around the camp while taking in the basketball courts and baseball field with the "once upon a time" resort complex and ocean fading into the darkness with this cool, balmy breeze making me wonder just what in the hell is going on here.

We fell out for roll call at 4:00am the next morning. Some were called out and sent to various parts of Nam wherever they were needed the most - but not me.

Whoever wasn't chosen went on different details around the base - which could be anything from just cleaning up to K.P. or painting. In the Army everything always needs a little paint!

On my second day, I reported to a captain in charge of the details. He assigned me to an area where Quonset huts, barracks, and mess halls were being built to accommodate hundreds of incoming troops. It was a bee hive of activity.

I told the Sergeant in charge that I was a union sheet metal worker and could weld. Word of this got back to the captain and I was told to report to his office that afternoon, ASAP.

Something inside me was telling me that this was not real, so I simply thought, "Well, Ken, just keep going and see what happens."

The Captain gave me a big smile and a firm hand shake and then asked me to sit and tell him about my history in the construction industry. Before I finished my third sentence, he picked up his phone, screamed orders at whomever was on the other end of the phone about my 201 file. He slammed down the phone and then returned all of his attention to me.

After I was finished speaking he said, "Am I glad you're here – Wow! This is great! I can't get an engineer to save my ass and none of 'em are worth a shit anyway. You got yourself a job, Kinsler - you ain't leaving here!"

It sounded like music to my ears! I was a journeyman foreman so I knew how to read prints and run a job from start to finish. None of my talents or abilities were taken into consideration prior to my infantry training, but my paperwork told the story of my life. I was not alone in regards to this type of oversight (as I was to find out in the cases of many of my friends).

I trained with lab technicians, college graduates, tool & die makers, professional truck drivers, etc. But there we were, walking around with 11-B-20 on our 201's. 11-B-20 means infantry small arms. The infantry is referred to as the "Queen of Battle" in that all other military personnel serve her - including the Air Force and Navy.

All the other MOS's and branches of military service are needed, valued, and are to be honored, but only 14% of our service men and women put guns in their hands and shoot people on a field of battle. The grunts are the warriors of the armed forces.

The Army and Marines compose the greater number of those who sacrifice their lives - and subsequently become the most needed in a "boots on the ground war."

Even giving the Army the benefit of the doubt, the above mentioned statistic could be a reasonable excuse for the misplacing of personnel, but in this high tech world of ours, I am not willing to give the Army any excuse for misplacing personnel.

If I appear a little cynical, it's because I am a little cynical.

You are reading this from the perspective of a grunt. My assessments and observations are those of a foot soldier who's not in charge of anything other than trying to save his own ass. And this is 1968 I'm talking about, not 2013. And Vietnam cannot be compared, in any respect, to Iraq or Afghanistan or Korea.

In penal institutions, it is their goal to reduce the amount of decisions an inmate makes per day down to twenty two. My experience in the Army fundamentally paralleled the goals of wardens or superintendents of prisons in their pursuit of creating well behaved inmates! If you get a human being (in or out of uniform) down to twenty two decisions per day, he will be totally manageable, easy to control, and will do whatever he is told.

In infantry training, they attempt to strip you of your identity and cut all ties to your past. They tell you when to sleep, when to eat, when to work, and when to play. You do everything exactly like the guy next to you - including shitting together in barracks toilet areas without partitions and shower in rooms which can accommodate 15 guys. There is no privacy. All of this is preparation for you to die together without questioning or doubting an order or hierarchy. We've all see it in movies like Braveheart, Gettysburg, or the famous Beaches of Normandy.

Statistically, the average amount of actual days of combat fighting with small arms in WWII was 10 days in the course of 365. In Vietnam, the number was 240 days in the course of 365. Just to give you a perspective by comparison; we suffered more K.I.A's during the months of the TET Offensive in 1968 than all the K.I.A's in the Iraq and Afghanistan wars combined.

Hollywood falls far short in its efforts to portray what goes through the mind of a man on a battlefield - except perhaps for a few scenes in Platoon or Saving Private Ryan.

It is not my intention to impress or convince you, the reader, but rather to simply convey my view as an Army grunt as it happened to me. This is a portrayal, a very personal appraisal - and I'm aware of the fact that you're hearing harsh judgment between the lines.

I wouldn't trade my 2 year Army career for 10 million dollars, but I wouldn't give 5 cents to do it again.

Although I had no knowledge of the concept at the time, I sensed that the ulterior motive behind my infantry training was to minimize my daily decisions. I fought inside to maintain my individual identity and dignity – which later proved to be a battle I had won.

I was willing to fight and die for my country, if necessary - while at the same time, I refused to embellish the war record of some misplaced, incompetent, narcissistic officer in his pursuit of another bar on his shoulder.

At any rate, my commanding officer was frantically trying to retrieve my 201 file so he could keep me in Cam Ranh Bay. I sat there in his office listening to him plead with a General to send my paperwork back from Pleiku, but to no avail.

The system prevailed (as usual) and sent me to the Central Highlands the next day. There was the right way, the wrong way, and the Army way. You did not argue with the "Big Green Bitch" as she was so lovingly referred to. Let me get back to S - my skinny little Jewish friend who had no business even being in the Army, let alone Vietnam. He was a great guy with a perpetual smile on his face and a beard that started just below his eyes and ended at his waist. S was hairy! He handled his 45 automatic pistol like you'd carry a dirty diaper to the toilet to wash it out.

S loved his country and was proud and honored to serve in Vietnam. Everyone liked him and he never complained. S was a model soldier except for one thing - he abhorred killing in every form. He was an objector, a conscientious objector - and that was okay with me.

So how do you swim without getting wet? How do you soldier without shooting a gun? Who knows - who cares?

S had a narrow face and head, so his steel pot looked like an umbrella on him. He carried his M-16 with one hand like you'd carry a pool cue as you walk around the table sizing up your next shot.

There was nothing not to like about S!

One afternoon, I watched him scribbling on the back of a C-ration box. He was just killing time (which was the kind of killing none of us objected to) by etching a helmet with a broken pencil that was lying on the ground in front of his hooch. There was also an M-16 lying on a steel pot, and in minutes he captured it as he etched it out in perfect detail.

I was amazed at his talent. Everyone was amazed at his talent - everyone, of course, except his draft board back home. S was no doubt the best example of the Army's inability to evaluate personnel. We were in stitches as he started drawing characterizations of all of us and we appreciated his gift. His artistic talent was noticed by our company commander and our friend was gone the next week - off to Brigade Headquarters to become the Brigade Artist.

S traveled with Generals and was stationed in rear areas to sketch whatever scenes needed the personal heartfelt touches a camera could not provide.

He was the exception to the rule in the misplacing scenario of the Big Green Bitch. His talents were used to benefit him and the Army. I was glad to see it happen and he was my friend.

We thought our power and might would intimidate the enemy. What we didn't know was the NVA's Generals were schooled on the fields of battle - and ours in the classrooms of West Point.

The NVA used our superior war machine to beat us and demoralize us (which is a concept taught in martial arts).

We were accustomed to the toe-to-toe battles in France, Germany, North Africa, the Philippines, etc...

The NVA fought like a bear in the woods. They would stalk us for days, watch our movements without our knowledge, and then toy with us before they would attack like a cat and mouse game.

They would retreat with a small force - only to ambush us with a large one as we would be drawn into a stock yard for slaughter. The NVA fought and picked their battles when they knew they would win.

We were bulls in a china shop; they were cunning, crafty and elusive. We were noisy and telegraphed every move with tanks, helicopters or artillery. We were Sherman's march to the sea. Our planes, ships, artillery and tanks killed many and won their battles. However, on the ground, in a man to man fight, we lost!

The motive behind Hollywood's portrayal of Vietnam was to make money, not to tell the truth about what really happened.

The only time the NVA initiated a firefight was when they had us outnumbered and in a vulnerable position.

Occasionally, we would catch them with their pants down, but only when we moved in small numbers so as not to telegraph our position.

You can eat your popcorn and be entertained, but don't drink the Kool-Aid because Hollywood did not tell the American people the truth about Vietnam. If you really want to find out how it was, ask a grunt who made it through a year or two, but chances are he won't talk about it. This I know for sure. The guys who sit in Starbuck's and brag about what they did in Nam never fired their rifles. Braggarts suffer from self-esteem issues and feel the need to boast - or they may simply just be full of shit about everything they have to say.

In the workplace, at the lunch table, the conversation will usually tear up the bosses' decisions and offer up a litany of better ideas. These are verbalized for 20 straight minutes over bologna sandwiches. Everyone with a better way to do things wants to talk and share their ideas.

On the battlefield, no one wants to be the boss. Fueled by the ineptitude in us or our willingness to abdicate the decisions that result in life or death, even the hard core atheist, without knowing why, will retreat from the decision, responsibility or business of when someone lives or dies. Because whether or not we want to admit it, something deeply spiritual lies in the birth and death of us all. The weight of such responsibility is seen on the faces of Generals who aged well before their years.

On the other hand, there are those who appraise life's accountabilities of such magnitude with as much consideration as you'd spend picking out your rental car at the airport.

My Grandmother used to say, "The dumber the farmer, the bigger the potato." I think that applies – or maybe not!

Trying to increase profit margins by reshuffling or downsizing the staff and cutting employees is one thing. Deciding who will walk point (knowing full well the average life expectancy of a point man is shorter than 18 seconds) is a horse of a different color. The result of a right decision in the green room will give the shareholders a profit and grow the company. The result of the right decision of who will walk point that day will fill a body bag. Right or wrong, good decision or bad - it made no difference.

How one weathers those daily decisions has a way of becoming the array of chemicals used in the development of a clear, sharp photograph - and daily command decisions will ultimately reveal the heart of a true leader.

Of course I didn't have a clue about any of this back then and I am only here today, 45 years later, as a result of prayer and instincts - as well as favor. I am, however, very thankful that I can see clearly now because the rain of Vietnam has gone in many ways. Make no mistake about the officers in Vietnam; they were trained by the military, but permitted to serve only by the grunts.

I recently watched a little 8 year old Chinese boy, whose feet could barely touch the pedals of his grand piano, play Mozart with the excellence of a seasoned pianist. However, if you closed your eyes and just listened, you could sense the lack of heart, passion and pathos in the ebb and flow of Mozart's lust for life. The kid missed not one note, but his fingers responded to the thoughts from his head instead of the passion from his heart. It was evident that he hadn't fully experienced the pain of life as well as its joys. The kid's performance was impressive at best, however, I don't remember his name. Perhaps I would have if he was able to identify with the intensity of life that only experience can give.

There was a resonating heart-to-heart connection Mozart wove into his music that you can feel inside - like when you listen to Frank Sinatra sing "My Way." We can relate because we've all been there.

It's about connecting - whether on stage, screen, music, a battlefield or marriage. If you connected with someone in Vietnam, you would take a bullet for them, whether they're an officer or an NCO. Then there were those who you handled like Al Pacino did in Scarface if you couldn't trust them. Remember his line, "You know what Frank, I think you're a cockroach" - then he shot him in the chest.

Vietnam was savage and holy, it was sweet and sour, creative and destructive, all at the same time. It afforded you the option and opportunity to connect with yourself if you wanted to or needed to. One doesn't read a Bible to find out about God - you read a Bible to discover who you are. Vietnam could do that as well (if you had the intestinal fortitude to honestly read yourself).

Vietnam was the magnifying glass you needed in order to find that tiny metal sliver in your index finger that you have got to get out because it's stopping you from doing everything you needed to do that day.

The battlefields of Vietnam prepared some men for life's struggles back home and crippled others who were late for the bell or refused to pick up the magnifying glass to find the sliver.

As much as I don't like platitudes, stumbling blocks can be turned into stepping stones.

The tough times as civilians make us or break us. If we stay awake in class, pay attention to caring adults, and if we're fortunate enough to have them, we experience the valid rites of passage in life. Then there will be beaches, golf courses, nice homes, and the autumns of retirement we dream about.

Conversely, the same rite of passage was there in Nam for the taking - only on fast forward, like time lapse photography showing the growth of a seven foot tall stalk of corn in 15 seconds. One 10 minute firefight was the equivalent of a four year degree in Interpersonal Relationships from Stetson University. Life is an open book test either way, but Vietnam required a little Novocain to get you through the pain of the things we all ultimately must encounter as we confront ourselves.

Chapter 11
What's Your Fucking Call Sign?

D was the guy you liked and didn't know why. He bragged a lot about everything, but you didn't care. He monopolized every conversation and always had a bigger, faster and older one.

D was a quintessential salesman whose product was himself. He was the kinda' guy that gave you that sick feeling in your stomach – like when you know you just made a big mistake driving that used Chevy off the lot and into the street. How could I be so stupid believing that used car salesman with his polyester sport coat? Well that was D, but you had to like him because he gave you no choice.

We all want to believe and trust the best in people - and D knew the secret of how to help you do just that (even against your better judgment). He was like a musician in a great symphony orchestra who, by himself, had no special significance, but is vitally needed to produce the magnificent sound that emanates from the Boston Pop at Radio City Music Hall. He also had a gift for creating wonderful music in our "symphony of life" – even during a monsoon rain when you felt like shit.

He had 8 months in country and was an RTO in the TOC where I was temporarily assigned. We had a mutual respect for each other, both having spent previous months humping mountains as grunts to earn our newfound positions as RTO's.

You had to take D with a grain of salt, but food without salt tastes so bland! So for a very short season, D became the spice in our otherwise boring C-rations.

The TOC we worked in was out in the boonies near Cambodia. I spent what seemed like a lifetime near the Cambodian border in the Northern part of II Corps. We had an artillery battery of 105's and a self-propelled 8" which had a habit of lifting you several inches off the ground during a deep sleep when it fired at 3:00 am without warning.

Engineers dug a huge hole and buried an air-conditioned railroad box car (which served as living quarters for our full bird Colonel who commanded our Battalion). The perimeter was secure, so we thought, with hundreds of troops and thousands of feet of barbed wire. As secure as it seemed, it did not insulate us from an occasional mortar round or sporadic small arms fire from doped up dinks who were trying to remind us we were not in Japan. But, compared to my previous time in the field, I could at least get a decent night's sleep once in a while.

During the daytime, our battalion was busy with meetings – as well as re-supply choppers blowing insane amounts of red dirt as they landed or took off. We also had to contend with the never ending stream of NFG's (new fucking guys) coming in from the states. And of course, there was the constant deployment of patrols and night ambushes. The dark of night came as abruptly as when the chief engineer trips the main breaker in the amusement park. It was against the law in the boonies to violate darkness with candles or even a cigarette. This forced us to depend on listening instead of seeing.

"Dark night from the eye his function takes, the ear more quickly of apprehension makes, wherein it doth impair the seeing sense, it pays the hearing double recompense."- Shakespeare

Night and day were as different as a walk through a Nebraska corn field is from a stroll in Time Square on New Year's Eve.

The fleeting sense of security enjoyed during the day left like a thief in the night as the sunset gave way to a moonrise that gave birth to varying shades of darkness which formed shifting shadows out of mists of moisture that seemed to be stationary - like looking at a landscape oil painting. D and I had earned our place in this semi-safe zone. We enjoyed the hot chow and beer, but deep down, we had a longing to return to the episodes that earned us our new cushy assignments.

Internally, there's something very weird and sinister about destruction that we all relish - like when we laugh at people who trip or fall.

We go to Daytona to watch 'em race around the Speedway, yet most of us hope to see a record breaking accident that sends tires flying into the nose bleed section.

After spending 30 minutes building a house of cards, we love to pull out the bottom ace - causing the stack to collapse.

Creation and destruction inhabit and inhibit us. They co-exist as we dare ourselves to get closer to the edge of our ultimatums. D and I conversed about this concept often. The green guys would listen, but never enter into our conversations.

I loved to build airplanes as a boy. I especially liked the ones that I had to cut out of balsa wood with Xacto knives. I would stretch colored tissue paper over the fuselage and wings, gluing first, then carefully painting with water which would cause the paper to shrink and get tight. Then I would paint everything bright yellow and carefully place all of the decals of stars and stripes - and of course, Betty Grable. The gas engine was next, complete with fuel tank. Then the antenna, and bombs under the wings and machine guns and rockets everywhere. It took months for me to build the aircraft, and with its 55 inch wing span, it was hard to get it up the stairs and out of the cellar.

I waited for a day without wind, and hauled up the plane to the porch on the second floor of my home. I filled the gas tank and cranked up the engine. I adjusted the flaps for a vertical climb, then I poured a half a can of lighter fluid all over it and pushed it over the railing in the direction of the Chevy plant three blocks away. I then lit the fuel with my match just before liftoff.

My masterpiece climbed and climbed hundreds of feet as flames poured from her wings. Smoke trailed behind her as she headed towards a colossal crash into the tallest smoke stack in the Chevy plant. And then she crashed – falling, twisting and turning onto the roof. It was magnificent.

I stood there all alone on my porch as I screamed and yelled, enjoying every second of the flight with a sense of triumph! I didn't need or want anyone there to share that epic event. The exhilaration of creating it with my own hands and then carefully planning her triumphant dive was an achievement I'll never forget. Something about destroying things was so appealing to me.

I got the same exhilaration rush when I fired a LAW (Long range Anti-tank Weapon) into a village and heard the secondary explosions. I watched as people, hogs and dogs frantically ran in every direction. The fire engulfed the huts and the sky filled with smoke.

Sensibilities and considerations are not part of your repertoire of options in a time of war. You either yield to them or you don't. You cannot reason with yourself when you kill because you are not yourself when you squeeze the trigger. Concerns are luxuries you cannot afford.

D and I were plane crashers itching for a flight, but scared shitless at the same time. He was a bit more anxious than I was though, so when the Captain called for a volunteer, D's hand went up and mine hesitated, just a little.

They needed a seasoned RTO for a platoon size 5 day hump (which was to be a re-con with orders to engage only if need be).

D was ready to carve one more notch on the handle of his 45, so off he went. I was working the graveyard shift in the TOC. The stage was set for the command performance.

During the night time shift, we would write letters to home, play solitaire, or read to stay awake. Situation reports would come in on the hour and we would monitor the weather frequency for changes while entering all of our activities in the log for the next shift and the morning meeting. Occasionally, there would be an artillery request for our 105's or for the 8" gun.

A huge, detailed map of our A.O. (area of operation) sat up on an easel tripod. The map was marked with different colored flags on push pins which denoted our night ambushes and patrol progress along with recent sightings of NVA movements and VC trails from past surveillance or encounters.

Officially, D was just an RTO on this patrol, but in reality, he was the only seasoned warrior in the platoon. Strategy and planning are useless terms when the bullets fly past your head. The only thing that will suffice in that circumstance is instincts gained through experience and D had them. However all of his experience was about to be tested.

In many respects, a small arms firefight was akin to a game of chess. Offense and defense can reverse with every move. A strategic three point move forward will be changed to a two point retreat when your gut feelings trump logic in a split second.

The definition of "bragging" changes if you can back up your big mouth - like when Mohammad Ali would say, "I'm the greatest" - and he was, because he repeatedly backed up his bragging in the boxing ring. D liked to brag too - and D could back it up as well.

The next morning, the rain was coming down horizontally, so they got a late start as a result of waiting for flyable weather for their choppers.

They had a cold LZ (landing zone), which meant no resistance, and moved only a couple klicks away before digging in for the night.

I reported in a couple hours early for my shift in the TOC. There was a brand new RTO scheduled to be my partner that night. This new guy thing seemed to be happening more often (or it could have just been me over thinking the situation). His MOS was a radio operator, so his skill with equipment and overall knowledge far exceeded mine. I was all ears and willing to learn and he afforded me a great deal of respect in spite of my lack of experience with the equipment. He knew my education with radios had been in the form of "initiation by fire" and he respected me for wanting to tap into his knowledge that he had acquired in the States. Firing an M-60 machine gun into a berm at Ft. Polk, LA is not the same as firing into a squad of NVA warriors rushing toward you with their bayonets fixed. He understood the difference. How refreshing!

So after updating the maps, checking our equipment, and reviewing the new call signs of all our elements in the field and posting them, we dealt the cards, got our cokes and cigarettes out, and settled down for just another evening of drama at the opera.

It was about 2 am when squelch broke on our radio - twice, then three times again without waiting for a response. This was unusual and out of the norm for me, but not to my new partner. What was about to happen was another one of those tricks not taught in a classroom.

I've heard an old adage that all cognac is brandy, but not all brandy is cognac! The same was true about breaking squelch. All squelch breaking is the same, except when it happens in Vietnam. Abnormal was normal, usual was suspicious, caution trumped relaxation and when you drank water from a canteen, you swished it around in your mouth before swallowing so you could spit out foreign objects. We dared not TRUST anything or anyone.

We waited for a call sign, but got none. What we did hear was a request for 105's with coordinates – which we quickly spotted on our pre-plot grid map. We waited, but still no call sign came. I responded by asking for his call sign. There was a long pause, and then the hair on the back of my neck started to rise. I sent another request, but again, no call sign. Nothing.

The voice on the other end of the radio sounded really pissed at me as he yelled to me about spotting a large concentration of NAV at this particular pre-lot - but again, no call sign.

"I want fire for effect, now! Or I'll get you court marshaled, you asshole!" the voice on the other end of the radio demanded.

My partner was alerting the 105's for a fire mission, but we had to wake up our officer for authorization to shoot. Our officer on the shift was a green Lt. who was only in country about 2 weeks.

Still, I had no call sign from the field. The Lt. came in rubbing his eyes and dragging himself into the tent. He asked the guy for his call sign. A whispering voice came through the speaker.

"I can't light my flashlight to see what my call sign is for today. We got Charlie right on top of us out here. You've got to start the fire mission now!" the voice urged.

The Lt. told our green RTO to walk over to the artillery battery to commence with the fire mission.

I jumped up to tell the Lt not to do this without getting a call sign from the field. "You don't know who this fucking guy is, he might be a dink, you can't do this" I pleaded with the Lt.

The Lt. threatened me. After I told him to go fuck himself, I ran out of the tent to wake up the Colonel to stop the insanity.

I told the E-8 outside of the Colonel's bunker what was going on. The E-8 went in and woke him up. He came running out in his shorts and headed to the TOC.

He grabbed the radio and asked the guy for his call sign, but he got the same repeated response from the field - nothing but threats. Then our Colonel let him have it!

"I don't know what university you went to in the States, asshole, but I want your fucking call sign right now or I'm going to call for some heat on your ass" the Colonel firmly asserted.

The response from then on was in mixed Vietnamese and broken English. They were yelling about Americans being in their country. It turned out that Charlie had overrun a small patrol of our men - killing everyone on the recon patrol. The NVA had an English speaking, USA educated dude who then tried to call in a fire mission on one of our own positions which was close to them.

The Colonel shook my hand and commended me for my actions. He told the Lt. to report to him first thing in the morning as he exited the TOC. My new green partner graduated out of radio communications 101, a la Vietnam, and we never saw the Lt again. Imagine that!

The next day, D's platoon leader called to report heavy troop movements in and around his position. They were trying to re-con only, but with thirty grunts moving through the jungle, it didn't take long before Charlie spotted them. D's platoon was greatly outnumbered in the ambush.

When D called in to report, we could hear a lot of firepower going both ways. D was cool, but I read between the lines and heard what was behind his words.

Our Colonel came in to take over communications again. From our end, we could all hear the heated debate in the field with D screaming orders at his people. "Calm down and tell me what's happening?' the Colonel said with a reassuring tone.

The NVA tried to rush them with fixed bayonets, but failed in their attempt to overrun the hill. Both sides suffered heavy casualties.

The Lt. got killed, so D took the lead by order of the Colonel. Two additional platoons were preparing to chopper out for a rescue mission.

The tempo picked up in the TOC as our Colonel shouted orders to everyone in sight and within earshot - both over the radio and in the TOC command post.

D was yelling now and all normal radio protocol was out the window.

"Take it easy, son" the Colonel said with authoritative sympathy. "Help is on the way."

"We're getting overrun here! Dinks are everywhere! We've gotta have fuckin' help right now! They're everywhere!"

The Colonel responded in his calm, demure tone, "I know son. I know - help is on the way. You're gonna make it"

D responded in a panic, "Who the fuck are you? You don't know shit. We gotta..................................!!!

Then nothing. Dead silence. Everyone in the TOC stopped talking. The Colonel called D again and again - nothing. Then he said, "If you can't talk son, key your hand set for me."

Nothing. All our mouths were hanging wide open. We stared at the radio as if it had somehow turned into a television. We were all waiting for it to show us something. It seemed like an eternity while everyone stood there just watching. The silence was suffocating us all.

Then something or someone keyed D's hand set and the voices of the NVA flooded the TOC. Our interpreter was relaying the gist of what was being said - until the Colonel

162

told him to stop. There was no need to go on. Not a word was spoken as we all left the tent with our heads down.

D was one of the greatest men I had the pleasure to serve with.

"Greater love hath no man than this, that a man would lay down his life for his friends." - Jesus

The drama that played out in the TOC was totally different from that of humping mountains as a grunt.

Too much information was being force fed into my already unstable mind. "Confused" would not come close to describing how I felt inside. While walking point and humping mountains, I had visions of a well-oiled machine that backed us up when we called for help, but now I saw firsthand how mistaken I was. In reality, we were just a bunch of High School kids who were playing in the Super Bowl.

Joe Namath and Terry Bradshaw didn't win games by themselves - and that was why my buddy D and all the men on that patrol were killed. One or two guys who knew what they were doing were not enough to win a firefight. By the same token, one or two NFG's could get everybody killed. Worst of all, by the time you finally knew what you were doing in Nam, it was time to go home.

One afternoon I watched a battery of 105's being set up in a firebase camp. Each gun was surrounded with a 4' high wall of sandbags as the guns were being anchored and adjusted. Two guys were setting up a 100 foot antenna to contact the FO's in order to establish the pre-plots.

There were five guns in all and the settings had to be established by nightfall. They were firing adjustment rounds and talking to the FO's (forward observers) when, instead of simply looking in the direction at where the gun was about to fire, the guys were only looking at the gauges and instruments. The antenna was hit with an H.E. (High Explosive) round which killed two men and wounded several others. How did they tell Mom back home about her brave son who lost his life because of a stupid fuck up?

I watched a young APC driver unscrew the brass cap off the radiator of his overheated track vehicle. He was leaning over the radiator when it blew - throwing him into the air and scalding the whole top of his body. He was guilty of just being young and dumb and probably had never listened to his dad warn him about waiting for their overheated Chevy to cool down before taking off the cap. His screams echoed in my dreams for years.

In the field, you didn't get to see all this senseless bullshit - turning the danger of walking point into a strange kind of comfort zone (which was manageable to some degree) because there was a measure of control when you're alone.

When walking point, your only concerns would take place in front of you. In rear areas, you found yourself looking over your shoulders and behind yourself constantly - and never trusting anyone.

Whatever type of mission you went out on, the less people that were with you, the safer you were. One Clydesdale horse can pull 900 pounds, two Clydesdales will pull 2,700 pounds. The concept is called synergy. When two people know what they're doing, they will do the work of three. So "the more the better" wasn't true in Nam. The more people involved, the less effective we were.

The shock and awe used in Iraq failed in Vietnam. We could not intimidate the North Vietnamese in the same fashion.

One hot afternoon we were walking through a field of tall, razor sharp grass with a battalion sized element of troops. Again, the idea was to show Charlie how big and tough we were. There were hundreds of heavily armed infantry marching alongside each other converging on a large city.

It took forever to arrange the move. We were only into it for an hour when our movement through the grass stirred up some kind of insects that began to swarm all around us. They bit like deer flies as they bunched up into swarms - weaving in and around us as we pushed through the grass. Those tiny insects made it impossible to even think about what we were trying to do. The entire plan was called off - including artillery and air support. So much for shock and awe!

From time to time we were given cushy assignments like guarding a bridge or setting up on the outskirts of a large city. We would check out incoming and outgoing vehicles on the main roads leading to the town.

There were also mini R&R details that were much needed after intense fighting. One such R&R took place outside the city Kontum - one of the largest in South Vietnam. We made camp a ½ mile outside the city and set up a road block on the north end of town. There were open, barren fields on all sides of us with clusters of tall trees that provided shade for livestock - and us too!

It was relatively safe because Charlie couldn't sneak up on us – and, unlike in the jungle, the breezes were unrestricted and free to flow. We pretended to be a little north of Miami Beach. We played with the little kids and passed out chocolate bars. Who doesn't like chocolate?

There was no need to dig in or even fill sand bags, so we simply set up our hooch's wherever we wanted, in no particular defensive order. So there we were, scattered around the trees, looking like pepper on a plate of scrambled eggs.

We were writing letters, drinking beer, and doing nothing on the afternoon of our 2nd day when all of a sudden, our little paradise was interrupted by the random firing of one round which hit one of our guys in the leg.

We called for a dust off as everyone locked and loaded. There was nobody in the open fields for miles in every direction. No one had any idea where the bullet could have possibly come from. It had to be a sniper way up in one of the trees (of which there were not many).

We decided to pump the trees with lead and M-79's. Branches, leaves and limbs were falling everywhere. We stopped after what seemed to be 5 minutes or so. Half an hour later, another round from nowhere found its home in the chest of another one of our men.

The Hueys were called in to strafe the tree tops with their mini-guns and rockets. Some of the trees were on fire now and some had fallen. Twenty minutes later, one round was fired again - hitting yet another one of us, this time in the arm.

We packed up and moved about 500 feet away from the trees and an F-111 flew by, firing its cannons and a cluster bomb for good measure.

As we walked back to the scene (which had transitioned into an inferno of downed, burning trees with the smell of expended ammo still in the air), we were greeted with one more round fired into our midst. Luckily, this one found its home in the red dirt of our Miami Beach Resort. Words fail me in my attempt to describe what we were feeling inside at that time. How do you fight a suicide bomber in a shopping mall or a Kamikaze pilot?

It's a mental battle more than a physical one. Taking the beach at Normandy - or a human wave coming across the DMZ in Korea is one thing, but fighting ghosts is quite another.

In our minds, the anticipation was more intriguing, or should I say devastating, than the actual battle.

Hitchcock did a half hour show which was an "on the edge of your seat thriller" about an alleged bomb on a civilian flight. No one saw the bomb, no one knew who the bomber was, or if he was even on the plane - or was it a she? Was it to go off at a certain time? No one knew. They just got a message about a bomb on the plane. The music intensified and the cameras scanned the faces of the passengers in the absence of any dialogue. The pilot thought dropping the landing gear might trigger the bomb. The co-pilot suspected reaching a certain altitude would set it off, but nothing happened. Hitchcock was a genius of intrigue, but he didn't hold a candle to the Viet Cong. That single dink, with a sock full of rice around his neck, perched on top of that tree, kicked the shit out of the infantry and the Air Force with a hand full of bullets and heart full of determination. We never got the gook and we had to leave the area.

My time as a grunt in the boonies for 10 months was turning out to be my get out of jail free card; allowing me to advance and be moved into some very unique situations. Call it serendipity, luck, or a blessing from above - I was ready, willing, and able to give up walking point and being a tunnel rat in my line company.

One of my gifts arrived in the form of an S-3 major fresh out of West Point. His name was G. First impressions are lasting ones and such was the case for my new friend.

This guy was a breath of fresh air and I knew immediately that I liked him.

He had broad shoulders and stood around 6'2." I told him not to smile at night because his teeth glowed like ivory piano keys.

Now remember, I was just a Spec-4 who was joking with an African American Major, but he laughed out of control. Then he slapped me on the back and hugged me like his momma hugged him when he left for Nam.

He had a great deal of schooling behind him and the Army invested a lot of time and money into this man. He was the most charismatic soldier I had ever met and he was an Airborne Ranger to boot.

He was a no-nonsense, get the job done kind of guy and he respected and admired seasoned warriors in a way that I had never witnessed before. He listened more than he talked and there was an aura surrounding him which made people pay attention when he did speak.

The only flaw in his resume was that he hadn't seen any action in the field. Because of this, the battalion commander, (the same colonel who earlier shit canned the green Lt. in the T.O.C.) teamed us up and made me his personal RTO. What a coincidence – or did it have something to do with thinking about snow?

I had just gotten assigned to the TOC about a month before we were introduced. My face still had jungle rot and cuts and scrapes around my beard. Band aids where common features on my face. To top it off, my 10 month old steel pot cover told the story of my stay in Nam with personal history etched around the hand grenade pins, bug repellent and tetracycline - all of which caught his eye.

He gazed at my pot for a minute and told me to meet him in his tent after I cleaned up and got some fresh clothes. He wasn't OCD, but he was a bit of a neat freak. After cleaning up, I entered his tent and was greeted with a hand shake and a cold beer.

G simply said, "Kinsler, I'm gonna pick your brain."

He did just that as he sat there all afternoon, listening and listening some more! I confided in him without reservation.

I spoke about what Nam was like through my own eyes. He wanted all the details - and I gave them to him! I even included the events which could have gotten me court marshaled with the Captain - or killed by other grunts. I shared reluctantly at first, then with open, unreserved confession.

The emblems of rank on our arms and shoulders disappeared as two young men, clinging to what they needed to survive, found each other in a world of racial bigotry and prejudice. We valued each other and celebrated who we were. In that moment, we conversed - uninhibited, as we allowed a few beers to loosen us up so we could be honest - if only for an afternoon. He was not aware of the racial problems that existed and was thankful for the heads up.

After our conversation and drinks, we played the Army game outside his tent - as it should be within the military with a show of respect to officers. But I will never forget that afternoon when we bonded. We became closer than two coats of paint.

Our headquarters Captain noticed our unusually close relationship, so he labeled us salt and pepper. The nickname became our "handle" on the radio.

We became a dynamic duo - even with our visible differences. We spent most of our time in Hueys - flying into hot LZ's and coordinating major movements of infantry and artillery along with air support. We functioned like a well-oiled machine, talking on three and four frequencies at once while communicating with the chopper pilot as well.

For me, there could be no margin for error. I had to anticipate his next move, his every move - establishing contact before he would ask for it. He listened to me as well, when caught in a firefight. I used the infamous line that was spoken to me when I first got in country on him, "Whatever I tell you to do, do it - don't think!"

The Major caught on quick. After 3 weeks and a few combat assaults, he began to walk and chew gum at the same time - even when the shit hit the fan.

I must admit, it made me feel good inside when he would ask me, in the company of others officers, during strategy meetings, "What do you think we should do, Kinsler?"

Booker T. Washington once said, "Nothing will benefit a man more than to let him know that you trust him." Mr. Washington was right.

One afternoon, two captured NVA officers were brought to my Major for interrogation. We had a good interpreter, but these guys were not about to say anything except their name, rank and serial number.

We were up against more than a language barrier. The East and West cultures differ in ways beyond description. The gestures, mannerisms, tendencies and traits were turning our job of extracting information into a nightmare.

Then suddenly, the Major called for a chopper to land at the headquarters LZ. The five of us walked up to it as the pilot turned off the rotors.

Major G continued to question the two officers, using our interpreter. They refused to give us any information that we asked for. I pushed them onto the chopper, buckled them down, and then hand cuffed and blindfolded each one. The Major pumped them for information again with no response. The pilot cranked up the Huey and took us up about 1,000 feet. The Major questioned them again, but no response. I took off their blindfolds. Their fears were louder than the rotors. More questioning, but nothing. I put their blindfolds back on after the pilot did some docking and weaving maneuvers. Then the pilot took us down very slowly, taking 10 minutes to do so until we got down to about 20 feet off the ground. Then we kicked out one of the prisoners. The pilot then went back up very slowly to 2,000 feet.

I took the remaining prisoner's blindfold off and he saw his buddy was gone. He opened up to our interpreter with all the information we asked for, without reservation. We couldn't shut him up for an hour.

His buddy just got a broken leg and my Major taught us all a great lesson about interrogation of prisoners.

Chapter 12
Metamorphosis

If you're intrigued and still following me in my effort to share the details of my experiences in Vietnam, then please stay with me (which is what I asked my wife to do for 38 years - and she didn't regret it). If you allow me to play psychologist, I'll try to explain why I've brought this up, for whatever its worth.

I mentioned earlier that I had waited many years for the starting gun to go off and allow me to begin writing. Well there was much more to the business of writing than I ever imagined.

The whole messy business of digging up the past led me into dangerous waters. The depth and turbulence of these waters resided in the bowels, undisturbed for decades. It was up to me how I navigated or ignored them.

My first caution or attentiveness was directed to not allowing my portrayals of Vietnam to be akin to that of a description of how big the fish was that I caught at the end of the pier last summer. Attempting to choose the right adjectives found me staring at my legal pad for hours, then saying, "The hell with it. I'm going to watch TV!"

Then I started to carry a very small notebook everywhere I went. During a conversation at Starbucks, or while I was watching a commercial on TV, a word or thought would pop into my head, so I would jot it down. Then an idea would come to me just before I would fall asleep, so I would jot it down. Thus began my journey of facing Vietnam; the journey of facing my giants and the liberty of sharing them with you and other people I will never meet.

All of those random thoughts, unassociated as they were when I was receiving them, seemed to fit perfectly as they suited the picture I was attempting to paint about the war. Letter by letter, word by word, the portrait of what Vietnam looked like through MY eyes came into focus.

Isn't it interesting how a bad day can suddenly turn positive with a simple handshake and a smile from a stranger? Complex problems usually have simple solutions.

Ninety percent of the time, the things we worry about never happen. A great acronym for the word FEAR comes to mind – False Evidence Appearing Real! If we train ourselves to just wait a day or two, we'll wake up to a bright, sunny day and a different attitude. This can happen without our input or control.

The effortless freedom to go back and write about Vietnam was not available to me for over 40 years, but it suddenly showed up totally unannounced.

The concept of writing took me back to a time when I had to walk through mine fields, terrified to put my foot down. My life depended on every decision I made, so when my psyche changed, writing about Vietnam became a walk on the beach. I was more than intrigued by the freedom and release that freed my every thought and my very imagination. All of my thoughts revolved around writing this book. I didn't want to do anything else. My house got dirty and I would forget to eat.

Granted, I am venturing into the realm where the motivational speakers and Sunday preachers play. But then, I've never been afraid of a challenge. This is precisely one of the reasons I went to Vietnam rather than Canada to avoid the draft. Life is about freedom - and freedom is not just another word for "nothing left to lose." It's worth fighting for!

At any rate, one of the dynamic metamorphoses that occurred inside me was a newfound sense of congruency.

I personally believe we are all three part creatures. We have a spirit, a soul, and a body to house it all. I am aware that this belief of mine (and yours if you agree) could lead us into estimating how many angels can sit on the head of a pin, so don't worry, I'm not going to go there.

I am not attempting to change your mind in an effort to explain mine. No, no, no - I lingered, waiting for connectivity in myself and I am doing it again right now in hopes that we will connect, as I did with myself, before you continue reading my memoirs.

By congruency, I mean that my thoughts were beginning to flow unrestricted through my whole self - spirit, soul and body poured onto my legal pad. I was unable to stop what I could not start for decades.

We've all said things and wished we could take them back; because after we spoke, we realized that the negative appraisal of the listener halted our willingness to continue.

This may come out bad no matter how I phrase it, but I came to a place where I really did not give a rip what anyone thought about me - and I still don't. It's how I spell freedom - even now.

This magical concept flooded my inner being and deepest thoughts concerning Vietnam.

Words crystallize thoughts as they travel through us. My desire to write wasn't enough to motivate me to do the task until I was able to allow my words to flow through my conscious and my sub-conscious mind, completely unhindered.

The other factor to be considered as a reader is one that our police deal with at the scene of auto accidents. Officers often hear discrepancies in the depiction of events when interviewing the witnesses about exactly what they saw at the scene.

My buddies on hill 684 may have seen things totally different than I did, but then again, you're not reading their book.

Bear with me as I go one step further. It is one of my hopes, that just as unrelated words spoken to me at Starbucks gave me the clarity I needed to express myself to you as a reader, you might come to grips with some of the issues that have held you back from being who you want to be, saying what you really feel or just being able to put your head on your pillow and go to sleep without being bombarded every night with the same old bullshit.

What resided in the crucible of my being were events I was a part of and ashamed of. They halted my freedom to discuss them, even with myself. I justified some of the events, ignored others, and put the blame on the Army for the rest.

The release was as subtle and unnoticed as a hair line crack in the Hoover Dam.

Ironically, the benign and malignant memories were cut loose together, so I abandoned myself, feeling clean or separated from my senses like the warm, weird glow of euphoria from the first Vodka Martini.

The words emanated from my "new self" along with the recognition of help through lines in movies and conversations at parties. This gave me the permission I needed to be myself as I expressed what Vietnam was to me - as it is right now sitting here in my birthday suit at my computer. Don't tell me you never walk around nude for hours at a time.

I was much relieved when the flood gates opened in my mind and invited me back to my legal pad, but then I faced the next giant.

How could I even come close to accuracy in my writing about what really happened over there? After all, I hadn't been successful in talking about it to anyone, not even other vets. It's too much, too big and too everything. But the more I let go, the more I received. I could now see what I once shut out. The plumbing in my mind was clearer than before.

If caterpillars could talk, how would they describe the difference between having twenty legs and creeping on a leaf one day - and the very next day flying about and touching whatever they pleased?

Metamorphosis is no doubt one of the most phenomenal biological transitions of nature. My metamorphosis was installing air-conditioning duct work in the Erie County office building in downtown Buffalo, New York one minute, then shooting people in the jungles of an Asian country on the other side of our planet the next. This, for me, truly ranked right up there as being one of the most radical transitions that's completely devoid of logic or reason.

The events in my year in Vietnam had no zenith. Each new day found me standing on a precipitous cliff - seemingly pulling me down and into the next day. I remember standing on a concrete wall while watching the Niagara River flowing by me. The current was very fast as I was close to the falls on the Canadian side. As I stood on the edge looking down, the deep, swift, icy blue water was drawing me closer and closer with a hypnotic strength I'll never forget.

So it was in Nam, where I was being pulled into the danger of each day while resisting its power to overwhelm me.

Chapter 13
Wait a Minute

Like a bowl of Neapolitan ice cream, the seasons on the calendar melted into each other without notice or appreciation of their uniqueness. Summer, fall, winter, and spring were the same

The geography rendered similar appraisals - without noting the unique characteristics of the mountains. Only those of us who paid careful attention to such things began to notice the subtle differences after a few months in country.

Some folks like to scoop only the chocolate ice cream out of the Neapolitan flavors of strawberry and vanilla. Others skim off a little strawberry, chocolate and vanilla on every dive into the bowl.

The terrain where we were dropped off on this particular mission was so unique that it was even noticed by the skimmers who paid attention to nothing.

There are three categories of jungle - single, double, and triple canopy. Single canopy afforded you a good deal of sunlight through the tree top foliage, double a little less, and triple was unbelievably thick, allowing very little light to penetrate. The bamboo stood hundreds of feet tall alongside the teakwood trees - and God only knows what else. All of the various types of greenery wove the webbed network which supported the vines and leaves - creating a blanket ceiling that allowed only the tiniest shafts of light to sneak through. The green ceiling of a single canopy jungle turned black in a triple one - even during the daylight hours. At night it lost all of its opaque quality and turned into a steel-like blanket. The term DARK is a gross understatement when describing the veil of darkness created by the ceiling in a triple canopy jungle. We could barely see our hand in front of our face on a moonless night.

Another noteworthy characteristic of the triple canopy jungle was the slimy black earth underneath all the rich, virgin green, armored ceiling above.

We couldn't think of a reason why any human being would ever come here - ever - and if so, why? Yet we were there, smudging up the canvas of what nature took thousands of years to paint with our piss and diarrhea.

All of the ground was wet and dark in color and laced with the roots of trees on the surface of a glue-like muck ground. Many of these roots would spring up and become trees themselves. There were worms, snakes, grubs, leeches and flying insects who thought they were in heaven – and they were all waiting to feast on our flesh.

Strange bird calls interrupted the monkeys' chattering and the humidity was 130%, if that's possible.

The bushes on the ground were hip high and sparse - giving us a welcome view of hundreds of feet in all directions which cut short Charlie's element of surprise.

My platoon leader told me I had the point and essentially elected me to be our tour guide that morning. I shed my ruck sack and L.A.W. as I walked up to the front. I was carrying four hand grenades, 20 clips of M-16 ammo and a machete.

When walking point, some of our guys preferred a 12 gauge sawed-off shotgun - others just wanted a 45 cal. pistol with buckshot rounds. I preferred my M-16. I was fortunate, I might add, to have had good friends who taught me the masterful art of taking the lead as a point man.

The machete in my left hand was used for cutting vines and I held the pistol grip of the M-16 with my right hand. I kept my thumb resting on the switch of the M-16, which was positioned on semi-auto, ready to be changed to auto if the situation demanded it. This gave me a reasonable sense of confidence and control.

The monkeys were screaming instead of chattering as they would swing from limb to limb. This "monkey business" severely impaired my ability to concentrate or discern the difference between their movements and that of the VC.

I flipped to full auto and fired a clip of 18 rounds into a group of monkeys - dropping three of four of them. This gave us some peace and quiet for a short time. Our lives depended on hearing Charlie, not monkeys.

The rain started at 2:00pm and increased the 130% humidity - essentially turning the steam bath into a tsunami. The excessive moisture wrinkled the skin on our hands and feet, making them look like dried prunes. Walking felt more like skating.

We had to stop every few minutes because guys would lose their footing and slide down the mountain side 20 to 30 feet before being able to stop themselves and regain their footing.

The elements were tougher then the VC. At times, we found ourselves hoping for a firefight so we could just stop walking.

Finally the call came to break for the night. The cans of whatever we tried to eat became soup as soon as we opened them because of the rain. This also diluted our appetites along with the beans and wieners.

We stopped on the side of a ridgeline of mountains, so the only way to stop from sliding down was to put a tree in your crotch as we laid on our backs with our heads pointing to the top of the hill.

I put thick rubber bands around my ankles to squeeze my pants tight so nothing could crawl up my legs during the night. I wrapped my head in a green towel - leaving only my mouth exposed. I put my steel pot on and settled down for a good night's sleep (which I got).

Nobody complained about any of the inconveniences of the jungle because no one would listen.

I was rewarded for a successful day of walking point by getting the honor of doing it again the next day.

One of the poisonous snakes we feared the most was the bamboo viper. They were very small, only 10 to 12 inches long. They looked very much like a little toy made of transparent plastic. They were lime green in color and would never be found on the ground. They hung in bushes and trees and would drop on top of our ruck sacks as we would bulldoze our way through the thick bush. They had small mouths, so most of the time we would get bit on the ear, or lip or fingers.

Their venom was as deadly as a coral snake's, so if you got bit, you only had a few minutes to live. I saw several of them, but nobody in my company ever got bitten.

There were also cobras and pythons, but at least they gave you a warning. A group of little kids chased a cobra out of the bush and into an open court yard one afternoon. They were teasing it with sticks while laughing and screaming when one of them came to get me and pointed to my M-16. The snake was a big one and he was totally pissed off. He raised up his head and fanned out wide while docking and weaving. I went to full auto and emptied an 18 round clip in him - ruining his afternoon, but bringing much laughter to all the kids.

Another day we were walking in line when our point man spotted a 6 or 7 inch diameter python lying fast asleep on the right side of the trail. He just called out "snake on the right" and kept walking. Every grunt after him made the same call to the guy behind him. We couldn't measure him (and didn't dare wake him up), but he was at least 18 feet long.

The next day found us in thick vine country. My forward movement was slow and pissing off the platoon leader, but it was wearing me out.

We nicknamed the vines "wait a minute". They were as strong as nylon cords and had thorns that looked like fish hooks. If you got caught by one, you couldn't move forward so your first words were "Wait a minute".

We tagged the lizards, "fuck you" because their calls sounded like "huck u" or "uck u" or something that sounded close enough to "fuck you" for us.

One night my buddy got bit by some kind of spider. He woke up with his eyes pasted shut. He looked like he had been in the ring with George Foreman. The swelling went down in a few days, so he stayed in the field with us.

Anyway, back on our hill of black slime, our next day was spent fighting the elements again - with no sign of the VC. Burning the leeches off each other with the quick touch of a lit cigarette was turning into an art form.

One of our guys got malaria. He was burning up with fever. We couldn't cut a LZ for a dust off, so they dropped a duffle bag of ice. We made a makeshift tub out of two ponchos, put him in and covered him with the ice. His temp was around 104 degrees and the ice kept it down long enough for us to cut an LZ for a dust off.

One of the most fascinating dynamics of the human machine is the eye/hand coordination that we all use every day without realizing it. We open the drawer in the kitchen without thinking about it. We look at the spoon and pick it up. It sounds simple enough, but the complexities of the simple action number in the thousands. Working at my trade as a sheet metal worker, I learned how to draw intricate wavy lines on templates, then cut the line with a razor knife to make a pattern. If you concentrate on the waves two or three inches ahead of where the point of your knife touches the line, and move steadily, you'll stay right on the line perfectly. Try it sometime.

In martial arts, when breaking an object with your hand, you are to focus several inches beneath the point of impact and concentrate on where your hand will be after breaking the object rather than focusing on the point of contact. The concept is to not concentrate on where you are, but where you're going. The volume and speed of communication between the eyes, brain and trigger finger became immeasurable for me. Potential energy transitions to kinetic energy in a New York second when walking point. When I had the point, whatever moved died. I was lucky for sure to have survived. The prayers of my family and friends played a major role in my return home, but it was a nightmare for man or beast when I walked point.

I open fired on bushes that moved ever so slightly from the most gentle of breezes. God help the monkeys that caught me by surprise. Snakes that were startled by my feet and shadows created by trees shifting in the wind became instant targets for me. I fired at what I heard (and what I thought I heard). Sometimes I fired just for the hell of it. If I was on the point, I was firing.

In my high school days, if you got in the first punch, chances are you would win the fight. It was the same way with walking point. The idea was to shoot first or become another victim of the eighteen second life span statistic. One hot, lazy afternoon, I spotted the movement of some bushes on a neighboring hill some four or five hundred feet away. It appeared to be Charlie, walking on a trail or path from south to north. I fired a little in front of the movement and a body started rolling down and away from the path pushing the grass down as it tumbled. My buddies joined me in drenching the area with bullets. We nailed five of them and took one wounded prisoner. Other than that little skirmish, we hadn't had any significant contact with the NVA or VC in weeks. So, after ordering a drop of food, ammo, and an extra order of bug repellant, we continued humping the same type of slimy, endless, black terrain.

One morning while waiting for a chopper that was to drop off food and water, we set up our typical perimeter on a mountainside that had very tall bamboo. Cutting a landing zone was impossible. The triple canopy foliage in the tree tops was so thick that the chopper pilot was unable to even see the ground, let alone us waving our hands. We needed water desperately, so we popped some grape smoke and the Huey bombed us with 105 canisters of water. The DuPont Corporation was assigned the monumental task of designing a plastic container that was able to withstand a 200 foot drop in the jungles of Vietnam. They all broke like water balloons. We weren't DuPont engineers, but we came up with the brilliant idea of filling the gun powder canisters used by our 105mm artillery guys for our water supply. The containers were air and water tight, so they worked great, except that they never rinsed them out before filling them up with water. So our water was laced with gunpowder. The trick was to put the water in your month while keeping your teeth together to sift out the gunpowder like a screen. After a few minutes of that, you finally just opened up wide, no longer caring about feeling the chunks going down your throat.

It was late afternoon when we stopped humping and set up for the night, so I went outside the perimeter on a LP with two other guys. We found a good spot to set up while one chopper was still dropping water and ammo about 150 feet from the center of the top of our little knob of a hill.

The memory banks of our brains log thousands of sounds - inviting us to enjoy the gentle breeze blowing through the screen door - or making our eyes go straight up when we notice a foreign tick, tick, tick sound when starting our car in the morning. The following event will prove my point.

We would often bet on how many hours were left on the rotor blades of Hueys. The rap sound would be distinctly different on blades close to the end of their useful life. The sound of the tail rotor on this Huey was being muffled by the main blades that were laboring, but not totally losing their high pitch whine.

It was turning out to be just another LP until the three of us looked at each other as we heard a familiar sound coming from the chopper that was trying to maneuver for the drop directly above our heads. We are usually comforted by normal sounds, but strange or unusual ones can instantly instill fear in us.

Our Huey was in deep trouble; first because its rotor blades had too many hours of use on them, and second, because he was too close to the tips of the bamboo.

This one scared the shit out of us as we looked up. The tail rotor was cutting bamboo like a weed whacker. He couldn't stabilize the bird and finally the tail rotor broke into splinters and went flying everywhere. It then turned over on its side. The main rotor looked like a circular saw blade as it cut a line through the thick greenery.

All this was now taking place directly above the three of us. We ran in different directions without hesitation or discussion. I took only a few steps before being restrained by a cluster of "wait-a-minute" vines. I shed my clothes, but could not get away from all the vines. I had some around my neck and face and I could feel the hooks cutting my flesh as I struggled. The Huey was coming down on top of me as I broke the last vine that was holding me around my neck. I saw the white faces of the door gunner and pilot who were strapped in their seats just before they hit the ground some 15 feet from me.

Small fires ignited immediately. The AK-47's were the next sounds I heard at the crash site. I cut the pilot out of his seat. He had a broken arm, but the co-pilot was dead and the cabin was now starting to burn everywhere.

The other door gunner was shook up, but only suffered minor cuts. Our platoon leader sent half our men to assist the rescue and put out the fires.

There must have only been a few VC who enjoyed our fuck up, because after we fired a few clips, the incoming ceased - leaving us with the familiar sound of burning woods and the pilot screaming from the pain of his broken right arm.

The results of my fight with the vine that day left me with a few little scars on my face. I can't help but notice the scars when I shave each day and I always smile whenever I hear someone say, "Wait a minute."

The evening clockwork rain snuffed out the smoldering fires and the morphine helped our chopper pilot get through the night.

In the morning, a Chinook dropped a cable through the green ceiling of foliage. The two huge rotor blades created a flashlight effect by sending blinking shafts of multi-colored light into the otherwise soundless, motionless atmosphere underneath the triple canopy. He picked up the carcass of the Huey and dropped a chair to haul the pilot out as well.

The only thing accomplished on our mission in the muck and mire of that Godforsaken mountain range was the total physical exhaustion of everyone involved. The heat exhaustion and heat stroke took its toll to the point that we all had to be extracted. We discussed the troops who suffered unbearable cold during the Korean War and we wondered which was worse as we headed back to base camp.

I spent very little time at base camp for a myriad of reasons. I didn't like it there at all, but I was looking forward to this visit.

When I first arrived in December 1967, we were clearing fields and using tents. Each brief return visit would reveal new buildings, paved roads, NCO clubs, mess halls, PX's and airport runways with huge fuel storage tanks. All of this was being built only hundreds of feet from a city that, for all intents and purposes, looked precisely the way it did two thousand years ago.

An ancient eastern city gave birth to a high tech western suburb without permission or a vote - simply because it was in the middle of the country. This seems to be something the USA feels is necessary in our feeble attempts to westernize our planet after WWII.

At any rate, the 4th infantry base camp was designed to be multi-functional for obvious reasons - and recreational as well. The intention was to create a home away from home where warriors could enjoy a hiatus without fear of being shot at. So much for the best laid plans of mice and men!

My entire platoon reported to sick bay on arrival. We had everything from lung infections to diarrhea. We washed the antibiotics down with beer and whiskey while watching the color of the water in the hot tubs turn from murky gray to brownish red as the dirt left the pores of our skin.

I got a haircut and a nice close shave with a new blade. Then I took a steam bath followed by a massage from a very young 80 pound girl who took a stroll on my back and butt. Her little feet relaxed every memory in my mind and muscle in my body to an extent, but her offer of beaucoup sex was turned down because I just wanted to sleep - forever. My refusal for even a "number one blow job" amazed her - and me too.

It took a few days for my digestive system to adjust to hot food and even longer for my ears to get accustomed to hearing explosions at a distance rather than close range.

The smell of cheap perfume and the sound of the Korean band at the NCO club in their rendition of "Like a Bridge over Troubled Waters" was hysterical, but they did their best and ignored our laughter as they crucified the English language.

As much as I tried to take deep breaths in and relaxing easy exhales, the urge to turn quickly without reason took control of me like a muscle cramp that hits you in the middle of the night without warning during a sound sleep.

The beer wasn't working and the whiskey just made me throw up, so I decided to stretch out on my cot one afternoon and stare at the roof of my huge tent as it swelled up and flopped down - answering to the demanding winds of just another sweltering hot day in Southeast Asia.

My personal war succumbed to the bell for a couple days, but the fighting was still going on. Not being a part of it made me feel guilty. My thoughts were stampeding. Fears of what I didn't know about myself were emerging as I tried to make sense of what I was doing there. This break in the action found me re-evaluating my relationships with my buddies in the field - and my friends back home as well. My cluttered up mind was attempting to sort things out now that I had temporarily gotten off the merry-go-round. I flirted with how bad things were and attempted to create good things in my mind during the lull, but then decided to leave such lofty endeavors to the poets.

I suspect there are aspects of explaining life that Freud, Jung and Adler didn't delve into. Example: Please tell me why a charcoal-broiled porterhouse steak tastes much better when shared with a beautiful woman as opposed to eating one alone. My thoughts made no sense. Why should such things as eating steak bother me now?

191

I looked down the row of cots in my unusually large tent and saw an M. P. with his 45 in hand sitting next to a very scared looking young, African American grunt in handcuffs. There were no jails with bars and such to imprison people at Pleiku, so if you broke the law, a personal body guard was assigned for transport until you would be shipped back home to Leavenworth, KA or taken to LBJ (Long Binh Jail). I wondered what he had done, but I wouldn't dare ask. The steak with a beautiful woman issue seemed more important anyway.

My daydreaming was interrupted by two of my newer goof-ball buddies who wanted to get drunk at the NCO club. Drinking on an empty stomach was unwise, so we stopped at the mess hall on the way. The 173rd airborne shared our base camp, but not our mentality. We were "legs" and they were "airborne," so it only took a few beers to produce the fights. We would take a bullet for each other when fighting in the boonies, but would not allow a joke about jumping out of a perfectly good airplane to go by without getting a bloody lip.

I found a neutral corner when the fight broke out. I preferred to drink my beer and watch the Saturday night rumble. The Korean band kept right on playing, trying to sing the latest Beatles hits. The blood and beer were mixing on the floor when the MP's showed up to spoil the fun.

We grabbed a couple beers and went out the back door. Later that night, someone burned the NCO club to the ground just for laughs. So much for enjoying a little R & R in base camp.

On our way back to the barracks, my buddies decided they hadn't had enough fighting. Let me just interject an apology of sorts here for my replay of these particular events.

It would require another book to explain, if possible, the changes in my heart and mind from then to now. Please know that I am no longer the man that I used to be, but then the same holds true for you as well, no doubt. I've asked for my forgiveness from God and man - and I've gotten it. However, writing about times such as these without using offensive terminology could be compared to watching the movie "Scarface" without hearing the word fuck - not to mention the fact that the Pacino in Scarface is most certainly not the Pacino of real life.

I have mentioned more than once the static between blacks and whites in Vietnam and I'm a little embarrassed to confess that I was an active participant, to some extent.

I know I am not under oath here, but by the same token, I am not going to give you, the reader, an opportunity or desire to read between the lines. In 2013, we say "It is what it is". I needed to clear the air and give myself some freedom to express without restraint - and I trust you've heard my heart by now, so no more apologies should be necessary.

Preparation is the key element in a financial plan for the future - or for an excellent paint job in the bathroom. This creates the necessity of setting the stage for what I am about to convey concerning the black-white debacle in Nam.

As we are birthed into ages and times not formed or created by us, we find ourselves having to contend with the ideals and beliefs that previous politicians and cultures adhered to as they passed laws and standards to live by. We're born into this life, sown into this world, just as the "Doors " sang about. So we find ourselves looking up to the adults in the room around us without the inner capability of correctly judging the rightness or wrongness of what we see through our neophyte eyes.

The first time we're allowed to go down to the store to buy a candy bar by ourselves our world begins to enlarge, but our beliefs are set in concrete.

"The evolution of man is the evolution of his consciousness and consciousness cannot evolve unconsciously. The evolution of man is the evolution of his will, and 'will' cannot evolve involuntarily. The evolution of man is the evolution of his power of doing, and 'doing' cannot be the result of things which 'happen.'" – Gurdjieff

There exists an axiomatic type of want in us all to be treated the same outside of our safe havens and accepted zones as we're treated inside them. Our bubbles begin to burst right after or during our first solo voyage beyond our back yard.

How proactively we opt to lead our lives as we adjust to the change in observing adults from a horizontal vantage point differ as much as our finger prints – especially once we mature. We either remember what Dad said about the policeman being your friend and how we should always call him "officer" or "sir" - or we don't; opting to form our own standards and conduct to live by.

We either go home after work or go to the bar and get drunk. Then we suffer the consequences.

We can treat women with respect and favor them - or treat them like whores.

Our free wills are doled out without measure or instruction manuals.

We either get our ass out of bed and go to work and show up twenty minutes early - or we can be the first one to be laid off when things slow down. I think you get the point.

Hopefully we will come to the place where we choose to disagree with some of the attitudes and actions we looked up to when we were 3 years old. But hey, it was effortless to unquestionably think they were correct simply because they were older and watched TV with us.

It goes without saying that the above is a gross over simplification of what happens to us all as our lives are played out - and this is, of course, only my niche on a huge subject. So...

The prudent rule of thumb is to maintain machinery to insure a quality product, but there does come a time to sell it all or throw it out and buy new. The issue here is not the desired result, but the machinery needed to produce it.

We all have a legal and moral desire and right to the pursuit of happiness as is stated in our Constitution. How we go about pursuing happiness has drastically changed since 1776, and it needs to. Again, our pursuits may vary in method, but are synonymous in their desired outcome.

The strife in life is evoked by the clash of a multitude of differing mindsets and belief patterns – like experiencing the ticking of the clock without the benefit of systematic adjustment and/or correction of our beliefs.

Being a chip off the old block is great - as long as the old block had his head on straight.

If I carried the prejudices of my Dad, God rest his soul, into Vietnam, I would not be writing this book right now. My point is, I decided to change the way I thought about folks who didn't share my skin color. This ranked up there as one of my smartest decisions I ever made.

I know I am milking this point, but for good reason. As a 72 year old grandfather, I am experiencing the age-old generation gap scenario with my grandchildren. We love each other to pieces, but struggle at showing how to go about doing it (which is a clear example of my point). How can anyone explain the 60's?

What we SEE is filtered through the lens of who we ARE. So our perceptions are jaded by the values we change or allow to remain - right or wrong, good or bad. Our sub-conscious conscience is not a judge and jury, but a sponge we either wring out or leave alone.

Plato compared our recollections to impressions on a wax tablet. Maybe he was right!

At any rate, back then I was straddling the fence about racial conflicts. As a 26 year old, I judged my up-bringing and rationale of racial issues to be wrong without knowing why. The deeply rooted biases planted in my mind during my single digit years eased out of me through my teen age adolescent phase. By the time I hit my mid-twenties, I was in the habit of treating people the way they treated me - without regard to the color of their skin. Evidence of this could be heard in my choice of words and eye contact with anyone not sharing my skin color. When I told someone about a friend of mine, I would say "you know Tom, that tall dude who wears glasses" - not, "you know Tom, the tall black dude who wears glasses."

I further discovered that people of color picked up on my inner acceptance and feelings of equality without the benefit of a conversation with me. Again, I have no idea how all this happened, but a little eye contact and maybe a nod of the head had a way of erasing what our ancestors fought and died for at Gettysburg and Appomattox.

Shakespeare wrote, "When judgments are a parcel of their fortunes; and things outward do draw the inward quality after them."

So getting back to the three of us heading to the barracks. The climate in our environment prior to that time was heavy with racially motivated altercations - without provocation or legitimate reason.

One afternoon some hot chow was choppered in. We formed a line and 4 servers were dishing out the goodies. My friend P, an Italian guy, was in front of me in the line. They had vegetable soup (which P really loved), so he asked the guy serving for a double portion. There was enough food to feed a whole company and we were just a platoon. The guy serving the soup was a black E-4 from base camp.

He was a stranger to us (as were the other servers). He refused to give P another dipper of soup - or even a look.

P said, "I don't want anything but soup man, so come on, give me some more!"

The black E-4 hit P with the 18" long stainless steel scooper, cutting him from the top of his forehead down to his cheek and into his chin.

The food went everywhere and we beat the shit out of all four black servers - and the black door gunner on the chopper that brought the food. The pilot patiently waited for us to vent our anger and then hauled them back to the base camp hospital.

An argument over what type of music was eating up the battery life on a radio or tape player would bring life threats during the course of the next firefight.

"If you hate a person, you hate something in him that is part of yourself. What isn't part of ourselves doesn't disturb us."
- Hermann Hesse

The news of race riots back home poured gas on the fire of minor disagreements that would normally die out by themselves. The fear of taking a bullet from Charlie was compounded with that of getting hit in the back from a guy who didn't share your skin color.

So the decision was made to kick some "nigger ass" in the barracks by my two Irish buddies who were full of beer, whiskey and bigotry. I didn't want any part of it, but I was with them in body (skin color), so naturally it was assumed that ours was a union of spirit as well.

It was about 1:00am when we barged into a totally dark barracks where everyone was sleeping. All the lights went on and everyone starting screaming and swearing - followed by the "fucking nigger" comments of my two fighting Irish men. Within seconds, it looked like a movie set at Warner Brothers. Bunks were flipping and razors were flashing.

My first companion, E, picked on a skinny black kid who was greener to Vietnam than his fatigues, but this little dude learned to fight in the hood. He held his straight razor in his right hand with only about a half inch of it sticking out between his thumb and index finger. E put him in a head lock and was punching him with his left fist, but the kid was systematically cutting everywhere he could reach - making long, wavy cuts on E's legs and back. E released him, so the kid cut him even more.

My other scrapper friend tackled a guy about his own size and was soon on top of him. He was banging this guy's head into the floor after taking him down with a piece of wood the size of a baseball bat which came from a broken bunk bed.

I was trying to run to the door and get out when a huge E-5 clocked me in the eye, then on the nose, then wherever he wanted.

I went down while trying to roll out the door when the kicking started. It didn't stop until he was tired out. It was the worst beating I'd ever had, to this day. He only stopped because he actually felt sorry for me. I'm sure of it.

It seemed like a lifetime, but in just minutes the MP's broke up the fight. I went to sick bay, along with a few others, to get stitched up. We all walked out with our bottles of pain killers and fractured egos.

I'll spare you the ethnic language as I am sure your imaginations can fill in the blanks.

The only empirical conclusion we all reached was to leave each other alone as much as we could. Back home, you may never see the guy you had a fight with in a bar again, but all the guys who fought in the barracks that night sat down to eat c-rations together the next day in the boonies. "Don't mean nothin" pretty much summed it up.

"Nothing good ever comes from violence." - Martin Luther

Chapter 14
Bad Karma

My perceptions (or unconscious awareness) of the progression of time in the jungle was similar to my state of mind when I launched into my career as a sheet metal worker. When I started my 4 year apprenticeship in 1962, thoughts of retirement didn't enter the picture, because that kind of thinking wasn't merited at that juncture.

The longest day of the year is June 21st, but we don't dwell on that fact on the 22nd or the 20th!

Future? Forget about that! I checked out my clips of M-16 ammo to make sure they were clean. I pushed down on the bullets to make sure the springs were free and clear. Then I cleaned the ejector/extractor bolt mechanism in the same fashion that I made sure my deductions for Social Security and Medicare were on my weekly pay stubs - along with my union dues.

The future existed without serious conscious consideration - much like looking out the window of a dining car on a train as you sip your vodka martini while gazing at the lush green landscape that's whispering by as you travel through the mountains of Pennsylvania without the thought in mind that your destination will invariably influence your present just as much as your past.

Time wasn't monitored by the clock - no more than the face of your watch is able to tell you how to think about what it's showing you or informing you as the alarm goes off.

After adjusting my ruck sack and putting a clip in my M-16, I went to full auto and wondered if I was in a field looking at myself in the dining car passing by - or was I in the dining car looking out?

My platoon was decreasing in numbers without getting replacements, but that didn't dissuade our asshole Lt. from volunteering us to take the lead on an assault at a hill near Ban Me Thuot. There was no point man on this mission; instead we got in line about 8 feet apart and began to walk up just another fucking mountain.

J was to my right and M was on my left. We did our best to stay at each other's side while moving to the top. The jungle was thick for some of us, and clearer for others. This posed a danger of not being able to see who was creating the sounds of movement at our sides.

We resorted to hollering at each other while trying to maintain a perspective on where we were in relation to each other as the terrain was steadily getting steeper.

J was smoking a Lucky Strike cigarette, and as he turned to talk to me, a bullet from the top of the hill shattered the freshly lit butt. J's mouth was now displaying a stub of flowered looking tobacco and paper between his lips. His eyes almost popped out from the shocking realization of what a close call he just experienced. We burst out laughing while the tracers were flashing through the bush, making lines of light that cracked past our ears.

We returned fire as we continued to ascend the mountain. Charlie joined in our shouting as we tried to stay alongside each other. A few of us got hit on the initial burst, but it didn't seem as though we were fighting a lot of NVA or VC on this mountain. With that in mind, our walking was turning into a slow, uphill run and our hollering was getting louder than theirs.

By the time we made it to the top of the hill, Charlie understood that he was either a mother fucker or a cock sucker - or both. From our new vantage point, we could see several VC running down the backside of the hill so we shot at them until they disappeared into the thick bush. Several were critically wounded and unable to flee, three surrendered, and we had a kill count of eleven.

When the firefight was over, J lit another Lucky Strike and we resumed our laughter. We drank a whole canteen of hot water to celebrate our victory. The three who surrendered were starving, so we gave them some c-rations.

They were shaking uncontrollably as they took the food, while staring at the muzzles of our M-16s in their faces. The hunger overwhelmed their fears as they gorged themselves on peanut butter and ham with lima beans.

Some of them were doped up kids who were scared out of their minds. They could not understand how the people who had just killed their friends were now feeding those who survived. We could see the bewilderment on their faces and inquisitiveness in their eyes. They didn't understand - and neither did we.

Their expressions turned into mirrors, allowing us to look through the windows of our own souls. This forced us to face the reality of what we had done on that mountain of worthless real estate. We were ashamed, but wouldn't dare admit it.

In Edwin Stars' great hit song, he was hollering just like we were with the lyrics: "War, what is it good for... absolutely nothin'... say it again..."

My year of horror was drawing to a close. The fear of actually going home became greater than the fear of walking point. I suppose it was because of the unknown aspect of how I would handle going home after all that happened in Nam. I knew what to expect while walking point, but a five degree December day in Buffalo, New York was looking like Pandora's Box to me now.

Battered wives keep themselves in hostile relationships for fear of what would happen to them if they called the police. It looked like I was leaving my hostile life and going home soon - and that possibility demanded a major catharsis. I felt like I wanted to stay with what was trying to kill me.

My M-16 had become a prosthetic extension of my right hand. I had a callous where a blister once resided in the "V" between my thumb and index finger caused by the rough part of the pistol grip. The skin on my sides, right above the hip, had indentations from the aluminum ruck sack that was rubbing back and forth as I walked. My steel pot and head liner felt like a baseball cap to me. I had adapted to find comfort in what was once totally uncomfortable. I was a chameleon, but not green.

I had successfully transitioned into the life of a warrior; but just as a frog will not jump out of a pot of water when the temperature is increased slowly and steadily, I was dealing with the insane desire to stay in Vietnam. This life had become an acceptable one.

Some of my friends opted to do another tour as a door gunner or a cook after a two week leave and quick trip home. A sweet bonus for re-upping for 4 years was the icing on the cake.

I received an offer from the Special Forces to go back home for two weeks, then off to Ft. Bragg to get jump qualified and return to Vietnam as a Sergeant E-6. My survival as a grunt in 1968 was sufficient evidence of my combat ability. It was made clear to me that the Green Berets needed people desperately.

Then a thought came to me out of nowhere - the thought of staying in for 20 years and becoming a career soldier.

For 11 months my mind was unencumbered, free to reckon with only one issue, to get through the day alive. Now the calendar abruptly turned my manageable mind into a stampede.

A lonesome thought reminded me of the last 45 days and I invited it to clean out my contaminated head as I decided to check the spoons and pins on the hand grenades hanging from my belt.

Like a boxer in the ring for the final round, I took a quick drink of water, shoved my mouth piece back in, and I pounded my gloves into each other as the bell rang for round 12.

I knew I had to establish a road block to that mental escapade after seeing my buddies take off the gloves too soon and go home in a body bag. The thoughts of home could hypnotize you into an empty existence - an existence out of your control. My thoughts progressed into daydreams, blinding my eyes from what they once saw in a timely manner into what they overlooked or ignored.

As a grunt in Vietnam, everything had to connect; your eyes, ears, sense of smell and touch - your thinking, movements, feeling and sensing are heightened in a way like never before. You get a one minute break in your neutral corner, but you never stop looking directly into the eyes of your opponent. You don't look at the crowd or your trainer, just your enemy. Your only desire is to knock him out. You don't win on points - and draws are out of the question.

The first day I walked point, I told myself over and over, I was faster than every dink in Vietnam, I was stronger than every mother fucker in Vietnam, I was quicker than anybody on two feet, and I had a better gun with more bullets that fired faster than any AK-47. This thought resonated inside of me when I walked - if you stick your head up, you'll be one fucked up gook. It got ridiculous, or maybe not.

I allowed or invited those thoughts to dominate from within me as I walked point, but I didn't care. "I'm better at this than every man in my company. Come on, I dare you to show your face, because you will fucking die today."

That kind of thinking is sick, I knew that, but war is sick and I was not about to walk point with the attitude that my life would end in 18 seconds. You can't allow yourself to care or think about anything other than what you are doing.

I woke up out of my slumber just in time. I mastered the art of putting the future in the future, stopping it from creeping into the now.

I could feel the re-connect coming together - fitting me into place like that final piece in the big puzzle. This was a welcomed comfort and it reminded me of my grandmother who had a passion for picture puzzles. She would buy the big ones with the smallest pieces. She loved it when I would join her at the card table in the middle of the sitting room. She always bought the landscapes of trees and mountains with hundreds of different colors. First we had to do the border, then work our way to the center. It would take days to finish, but when we were close to the end the pieces were easier to place. Then we would hurry, trying to be the one who gets to finally fit in the last piece.

I knew I could not go home right then any more than we could complete a puzzle in one day, but we knew it would happen - and I knew I would go home. I would not allow myself to be anxious until I boarded that 707.

Whatever would happen when I got home would happen. So I decided I would just put another piece of the puzzle into the top corner with my Grandma and fall asleep.

In my 11th month in country, I had settled in as an RTO in a battalion TOC, but I was still watching over my life - just as a mama bear guards her cubs.

I was no longer walking point or going out on search and kill missions, but the slightest inclination of a perilous situation would spark my survival instincts. Keeping a lasso on my wandering mind proved to be the greatest challenge that I faced during every waking hour.

My Dad taught me how to drive when I was 16 years old. He told me that everyone on the road is stupid and that I had to drive for them. I was to watch them all the time and pay no attention to my own driving abilities. He said that accidents happen when people do stupid stuff and "you are not stupid." My dad would not wave at a friend that was walking by when he was behind the wheel. He would wait to stop at a signal before changing the volume on the radio. My dad would not turn his head to talk to my Mom who was sitting next to him while he was driving. When he was driving, that was all that he did.

My Dad also trained me how to be a combat infantry man with that lesson. I was not aware of that at the time, but being present in the moment will insure the presence of the next moment.

Who among us speaks about the benefits of a proper upbringing (or the lack thereof) to anyone besides themselves? How often do we, on purpose, even consider the above during the course of a normal day? Rarely if ever, would be my response.

What does my Mom's emphatic and persistent teaching and checking up on how I wiped my ass have to do with my tour in Vietnam? Well we were issued very small little packets of toilet paper in our c-ration boxes and I was

208

always asking my buddies for more paper and more paper – I was driving 'em nuts! When my butt was sore from diarrhea, I would drown it in Vaseline. Because when you are walking point, if your concentration is interrupted by a sore ass, you will die. My Mom taught me more than my Drill Sergeant about survival in Vietnam.

I had a baseball coach who was a broken record with his screaming to us in the outfield, "Keep your head in the game!", "Quit playing with the grass!" and "Wake up out there!"

I could hear my second grade teacher, who I was in puppy love with, tell me that I was doing a great job making the decorations for the Thanksgiving Day dining room table for my Mom.

I felt the warm affirmation in my heart when my principal handed me my diploma and shook my hand. The taste of Ivory soap is still in my mouth for calling my Mom a son-of-a-bitch when I was 9 years old.

Those events of embarrassment, pride, courage and shame molded my character – and miraculously remained in me in spite of all the olive drab clothing on the outside of me or the brainwashing the Army subjected me to in the attempt to alter the inside of me.

I was ordered to fight in this war by President Johnson. To me, it was no different than when my Dad ordered me to take out the garbage.

When a General's jeep passed you by, you saluted it, even if the General wasn't in the jeep. You saluted the stars on the bumper because they represented the man.

You see, I was living by a code of conduct not found in a military manual. Dominating forces that were developed during my quarter century of life were erupting to the surface into the atmosphere of wherever I was.

These kids all around me were dying because they were in diapers, not because they were bad soldiers. They were lions dying in zoos rather than in Africa.

My Dad told me I was not stupid, so I was not going to die because I was driving through an intersection of stupid people or marching through a jungle with stupid soldiers who were being led by stupid officers in a stupid war that was started by a stupid President and a stupid Congress.

If anybody was going to go home, it was going to be me! I came there alone and I would go home alone, but by God, I was going home - because I was not stupid.

My mind was highlighting the route on the map of my life. My navigation systems were the people who profoundly influenced me while growing up. My course corrections were being conducted by an unconscious cavalcade of characters - both friends and foes, who were affording me the simplest answers to the most complex problems that were not related to each other in any way, shape, or form.

I mean, what does checking the head space and timing on a 50 cal. machine gun with your "Go or Not Go" spacer have to do with putting all your crayons away in the box in the right sequence before you go to bed?

How could I thank my high school drama teacher, Mr. Gutta, at Kensington High School in 1958, for patiently waiting for me to remember my lines and then teaching me how to adlib while I am trying to recall them? Then he would skillfully incorporate my blunder into being a vital part of my character - all this without any help from the director.

So what does that have to do with changing how deep you dig your fox hole or how to fix a jammed up M-16 in the middle of a firefight that your platoon is losing? I don't have the answer, but the thought of simply grabbing the M-16 off of my buddy who just got shot instead of wasting a second trying to fix mine came to me in a nanosecond.

Thank you Mr. Gutta; your patience and determination to teach me in high school saved my life in Vietnam.

Most of us have either seen movies or read about what men do when locked up in solitary confinement for years on end and what they force themselves to do in order to save their minds. I read one account of a Navy pilot in a Japanese prison camp who built his home step by step, all in his mind while in captivity. He began with digging the hole for the cellar by hand. He then filled wheel barrels and envisioned every step of the construction. He ended by creating the exterior landscape. This pilot drove every nail, laid every brick, did all the plumbing, electrical, air conditioning, roofing, painting, and even hung every picture in his mind just as he imagined his wife would oversee and approve. It took five years to complete and proved to be the means to a happy ending. He survived the inhumane treatment of that prison and returned home into the arms of his loving wife. Once home, he actually built that dream home he created in his mind - without any blueprints.

Upon re-reading my effort, I have noticed a repeated rhythm, if you will. A rhythm where I write about an event on some hill, followed by a page or two about my appraisal of life lived back home or something to that effect.

It appears to me that my thoughts and rationalizations of home or the people in my past were the nails, wires and shingles that my comrade used to retain his sanity as well.

Often times, I told my friends that my two year hitch in the Army was like being in a prison without bars. They own you, you are the property of the USA just as much as the White House is.

I felt an invasion of privacy and a loss of individuality in a very tangible way - and I hated it. I could no longer connect the dots and my invisible prison felt as real as my Navy comrade's cell. Certainly I am not comparing his horrible suffering to mine, but many of the folks we know today live behind bars as well. Some are of their own making - and others, well you know what I mean.

I said all that to say this - I am not writing the thoughts presently in my head; I am penning what I thought about back then, during Vietnam's routine in 1968! Our minds are amazing.

One of my favorite people in the whole world is my Aunt Helene. She is my Mother's sister. Aunt Helene lives in

Washington State, so I don't get to see her as often as I would like. We talk on the phone now and then. She is in her 80's now, but her voice is exactly the same as when she was 17. It's almost scary when I talk to her because I feel like I've entered the twilight zone.

My remembrance of Vietnam has the same clarity as my Aunt's voice - in spite of all the years that have passed. Memories of Nam are vibrant and alive in me, though my depictions of Vietnam are as weathered as my Aunt's skin, they are as crystal clear as her warm, tender and youthful voice was over the phone last week.

My memories are less like a movie (which is a permanent emulsion of chemicals on celluloid) and more like a Broadway play in that they're subtly different each time it's performed; ergo what took place on April 16, 1968 is as securely fixed in my mind as the events on April 16, 2013 - the only difference being a newly acquired vocabulary with different adjectives.

The layered learning I spoke of earlier of eleven months in country still left me without comprehension or control of the big picture of war between countries; whether they be conflicts of ideology, religion, or at their core, simply about money. Nevertheless, I was injected with this uncanny notion of being able to control my little portion of chaos where I was forcibly stationed not as an observer who was listening to Walter Cronkite in my living room, but as an active participant who was getting shot at.

This God-sent revelation came through the door early in my one year tour of duty. The revelation became a welcomed life line of manna that arrived fresh every morning. This freaky micro-management of life set in, stemming from some unknown foreign source, yet it was welcomed in the same way that the state of normalcy yields to the antistatic as you are being gurney-driven into the operating room.

My year "under the influence" sustained me without regard to the intensity of what each day offered.

Just as I didn't understand why birds were flying over my head, I was able to stop them from making nests in my hair. Each day presented me with what I needed to get through that one day and into the next 24 hours of euphoria. Now if you can figure that out, you're a better man than I, Gunga Din! All I know is that I knew when the anesthesia was working and I knew if it was wearing off before the surgery was completed.

Optimism took courage when it was singularly focused on survival for that day, but now my scope of the future was extending beyond the date of leaving country - and not just the day I woke up to.

We all knew there would be no ticker-tape parades down Main Street for our homecoming. Before I was drafted I had seen the way returning soldiers and sailors were spit on in airports. I wasn't sure how I would handle that, but that would not require courage - not after Nam. I wondered if I had what it would take to survive after the homecoming.

Going back to work would take courage. Driving an automobile would take courage. Eating in restaurants, sleeping on sheets, and peeing in a toilet would all require courage.

I was down to 12 days and a wake up when a frustrated 1st Lt. entered our tent to escape a monsoon rain. He wanted a volunteer for a night ambush. He needed one more guy with radio experience.

If no one would volunteer, they would simply randomly pick out one of us who was playing cards, lying on a cot, or sleeping.

I shook my head in disbelief, but sure enough, it was the Yankee hating Lt. from Fort Polk, Louisiana whom I had greeted on the LZ some two months ago. He was walking into my life one more time. I was shocked to think he was still alive, but there he was coming right toward yours truly.

As he stood in front of me, I thought how easy it would be to just lift up my M-16 (which had a clip in it) and empty it into his chest, then spend the rest of my life in prison. Then I contemplated how I could do the same thing to him during a night ambush, if he picked me, and not go to prison.

I looked into his eyes and realized he was reading all of my thoughts. He remembered! I saw it on his face. He knew how he had treated me back in the States. I was reading his mind and exposing mine at the same time.

I didn't nod or say hello. I just stared into his eyes without blinking as all my thoughts about him at Ft. Polk came back. All the running backwards in front of me, all the Yankee slurs, all the calling me Gramps, all the "you poor old guy, I bet your legs are killing you with all that arthritis, you ol' fucker" and "we're going to send you to an Army nursing home with all the old soldiers." Everything came racing back into his memory like rewinding an old film.

He was watching how he treated me in AIT on the screen of my eyes like the credits that roll down at the end of a movie and seem to never end. My M-16 was lying across my knees as I sat on the edge of my cot. I kept my eye contact.

I flipped the selector from semi to full auto - and then back and forth, back and forth while maintaining eye contact with him. I didn't blink. The credits were still rolling down the screen, but now they were showing the script of what would transpire on this ambush when I was walking behind him (if he ordered me to go). The sound of the clicking got louder as my buddies next to me picked up on what was happening between us. They all smiled at him.

His mouth opened and his eyes flared out as if he was watching the birth of his child in the delivery room. Then suddenly he knew in his heart that he would never again see his son or go home alive if he ordered me to join the ambush. In only a short time, he had learned the do's and don'ts that would insure his longevity. So he put his head down, walked away, and ordered the guy on the next bunk to follow him.

Like one, that on a lonesome road
Doth walk in fear and dread,
And having once turned round, walks on.
And turns once more his head;
Because he knows a frightful friend
Doth close behind him tread.

~ Samuel Coleridge ~

Chapter 15
Home is Not Where the Heart is

I struggled with the thoughts of going home. My mind was spinning. Memories were bombarding me. My bearings were gone again. My draft notice was coupled with a cancellation of all my expectations as a civilian. For me, once in the Army, life itself went into a "limbo state of existence" - which was a kinky kind of relief. I didn't have to support myself in any way. I was promised 3 hots, a cot, and a paycheck every month. I didn't have to support anyone else. If I got sick, it wouldn't cost me anything for the best medical attention money could buy. I had no need of an automobile or any insurance.

All my worldly possessions could fit into one sandbag. I sold my car before I left, and none of my old clothes fit me anymore, so they were given away. It was like George Bailey's answered prayer when he wished he was never born in the Christmas movie "It's a Wonderful Life."

The change in weather graphically signaled the beginning and ending of the seasons in Buffalo, so our concept of "marking time" was a constant part of everyday conversation at work and at the bars. In Nam, that was in limbo too - because every day was hot. Who needs a weatherman in Vietnam? Nobody!

My personal and private dreams of life ended with my divorce. Yes it is true that my girlfriends were great in bed, but that's all they seemed to be.

They had passed a law that employers had to re-hire anyone who was drafted, so the only guarantee I had was my old job back home. The problem was that my hands were now accustomed to breaking things, not making things - so even that was all fucked up.

> *"How like winter hath my absence been*
> *From thee, the pleasure of the fleeting year!*
> *What freezings have I felt, that dark days seen!*
> *What old December's bareness everywhere."*
> *William Shakespeare*

How did Shakespeare know that I had arrived in December and would also leave in December?

I thought my buddies were crazy, but now I was beginning to understand why some of them were re-upping. Shouldering the many responsibilities of being a husband, father, bread winner and a taxpaying citizen was being trumped by the illusion of shooting people or training others how to shoot people for twenty more years as a career was now an option. Re-upping did have its financial rewards, BUT - twenty years of this?

In my two years of service, I failed to meet a "lifer" who played with a full deck. I am sure there are some, and hats off to them, but let's just say they're a different breed of cat. So there I was standing on a beautiful, white sand beach on this sunny afternoon with a cool, salty breeze blowing through my hair as my feet were sinking a little deeper into the sand with every little oncoming and outgoing wave. The sun was setting and its heat was gradually decreasing, making my shadow longer and longer as the sweat on my body was replaced by little chill bumps. I wasn't tired, thirsty or hungry - I was just there, suspended in time with all the insanity of life around me - without being in me.

There was nothing in front of me with the exception of the blue-green water which flowed into an even bluer sky that was accentuated with lazy white clouds that transitioned into shades of gold as the last rays of sunlight radiated from behind me as the sun plunged below the horizon.

I wanted to stay there, right in that spot, for the rest of my life. Then, out of nowhere, my 1st Sergeant's words made me jerk my head around.

"Kinsler, they want your ass in Plieku ASAP to do all the fuckin' paperwork. You're going home, dude."

When he said that, I saw a tsunami rising, as it swelled up into the sky. A mountain of water was rushing toward my peaceful beach. It went as far as my eyes could see, north and south, and I was arching my neck back to look at the top of the swell. I could not do anything to stop what was coming at me.

I had control of my circumstances for one whole year, but now I was going to be controlled by them. "More tears are shed over answered prayers," so said Truman Capote.

My subterranean thought patterns rose to the surface of my present state like a submarine's periscope pierces the surface of the deep without affecting it in the slightest.

My non-existent future for one year was now coming toward me like a fast freight train screaming through the middle of Chicago at midnight.

I was scared shitless to go home, but could think of nothing else.

Checking out of hotels has a way of being a pleasurable experience as we leave all our change and a $10.00 bill on the bathroom counter top. Then you take care of your bill at the front desk and check out the plane ticket in the breast pocket of your sports coat - all the while, your thoughts are riddled with going home to a house that needs to be freshened up after being unoccupied for two weeks while you were away. But I was trying to check out of the Limbo Hotel - and the destination on my ticket home was blank. This business of going home was no fun.

I gathered up all my stuff (which took all of two minutes). My buddies insisted we chug a few hot beers before I went out to the LZ to hitch a ride out of our firebase (which was close to Laos). I looked at my Timex watch and I was amazed at my newfound appreciation of time.

It was about 2 o'clock and the activity on the pad generally slowed down about 5 o'clock. We were re-hashing the past and recalling the play by play of firefights, my Dad mailing me whiskey and all the fun times we spent together on this hill and that bridge - and on and on.

When I wasn't talking, the concerns about not getting a ride off the firebase were starting to flood my mind. Hitching rides on helicopters was the same as holding out your thumb on I-95. There were no schedules available and it was up to the pilot if he wanted to let you on board.

We all jumped to attention when we were abruptly interrupted by some small arms fire on the opposite side of our firebase hill. Then a few mortar rounds hit, putting us into general quarters mode. The 105's were cranking up as the coordinates for the mortars were being located. They were firing for effect as the firebase geared up to prepare for an attack by the NVA.

I grabbed my ruck sack and M-16 and ran to the LZ where the last Huey was about to lift off. I caught the pilot's eyes and screamed over the roar of the engines, "DEROS" - which meant Date Eligible for Return from Overseas. The pilot didn't hear my words, but he read my lips as he gave me the nod to jump on board.

We got up to about 500 feet and could see 50 or so NVA creeping up to the perimeter on the opposite side of where I was with my buddies. The door gunner opened up with his machine gun and I joined him - emptying one clip after another with my M-16 as a little goodbye gesture to the North Vietnamese Army who were uninvited guests at my going home party.

I nestled my ass into a cluster of wooden boxes of paperwork with guys I had never met. Memories of a year ago kicked in with my first flight on a C-130. I was headed to Pleiku to begin this year of madness. I remembered an Air Force Sergeant who came out through the pilot's door and announced to the 30 of us, and the jeep on board, that we were going to be flying at a high altitude to avoid small arms fire. He also informed us that this was a flight which would take one and a half hours - all of which was over enemy territory. Then he said that if we have to ditch, "it's every man for himself." Mind you, none of us had been issued any weapons at that time. He continued his welcome speech "'I have the only weapon on board," as he pointed to his hand gun. "Welcome to Vietnam." He then turned around, went into the cabin and slammed the door.

My chopper docked to the right to avoid the small arms fire which was now being directed at us as the firebase below was consumed in red dust. We heard bullets hitting the aluminum skin of our Huey. He took us up to several thousand feet where the air was clean, fresh, and quiet. The mountains became innocent and beautiful again. We all looked at each other, shared smiles, and nodded our heads up and down. We sat there with our dirty faces and hands, acting like we were on a bus going home after a long day of work at the steel mill.

In December of 1967, my base camp at Pleiku was a beehive of bulldozers, cranes and stacks of building materials. Everyone was chasing their tails. My aerial view, now one year later as we approached our LZ, resembled one of those numbered slots you would see on the tarmac at O'Hare airfield in Chicago.

The concertina wire surrounding the base was so thick a mosquito could not get through it. The outskirts of the complex extended beyond vision as we descended into a replica of Rome, Italy with all the asphalt paved roads radiating out of its center.

The only familiar aspect of this return voyage was that of loneliness. No one was guiding you or telling you where to go next or what to do when you get there. The first time I came to Pleiku was as a replacement, not part of a unit. So before you get to where you have to be by 1300 hours (or whatever), you go through an average of 5 or 6 "How the fuck do I knows" when asking for directions or help.

My initial observation on this trip was that I had become a nuisance. The few of us who were able to walk after a full year as a grunt in the boonies were a pain in the ass to the career people who spent their 20 years behind desks.

The process of arriving in country involved classes about how to treat civilians as well as the do's and don'ts of political correctness and the history of why we were there in the first place. They corralled us into groups of 20 or so and we went from building to building quite smoothly. The returning groups in country were reduced to one person - YOU! You were treated like a piece of shit they had to get rid of. I guess this was in preparation for our welcome home experience that was soon to follow.

There were no handshakes, smiles, or thank yous, for a job well done. We were cattle - herded back and forth in the stock yards of Fort Worth. We were together and separated simultaneously.

The paperwork was endless, but at the end of the day, we could get drunk in the NCO Club or shop at the PX where they sold Rolex watches for $5,000.00 or a Baby Ruth candy bar sitting next to it for a dime. "What in the hell is going on here in this zoo?" I thought.

If you got unlucky or fucked up in some way, you went home in a body bag - or if you were wounded, you were a hero, but if you did your job well and survived, you were an asshole and you were treated like one. Killing your fair share of people and doing what you were ordered to do earned us the role of the red-headed step child.

We had a few hours of down time on the second day, so a group of us were told to fall out of our barracks and actually do a police call of the grounds. This meant picking up cigarette butts and whatever trash was lying around.

We could not believe what was happening. A milk toast E-6, fresh from the States, was in charge of this fiasco detail!

I befriended a guy named R who was an E-5. This was the end of his second tour, having served his first with the 1st Cav in 67'. We formed a solid relationship in one day - which was the kind that could become a lifelong friendship if given the time. R was a black guy, but his skin, already dark, had deepened into a penetrating blue-black onyx color as a result of the years under Vietnam's intense sun (which may or may not have anything to do with what you're about to read).

R had just been awarded a silver star for saving the lives of his squad by singlehandedly assaulting a large number of NVA with an M-60 machine gun. This he did of his own accord without being ordered to do so. He also had two Bronze Stars, an Army commendation with "V" device, and two Purple Hearts. His chest was covered with medals and his heart was as big as a hotel.

The two of us were shaking our heads in disbelief of what we were being commanded to do after surviving a year in the jungle. We were laughing as we walked out of the barracks and got in line. Finally R said, "No man! I ain't fuckin' doing this shit!" Then I told the sergeant to "go fuck himself" when he ordered us to pick up all the garbage on the grounds (and by the way, we were wearing dress khakis).

The E-6 pointed to his stripes and said, "You will do it because I have superior rank and I'm commanding you to pick up these butts!"

R's response was priceless, "You can kiss my black mother fuckin' ass."

The E-6 approached him (which was a bad mistake). R hit him with a right cross that broke the E-6's nose and knocked his teeth into and through his lower lip. His khaki-dress short sleeved shirt was slowly turning crimson red as the MP's arrived.

We all had to report to the S-3 Major to give our account of what happened. R could have gotten a couple years in military prison and a dishonorable discharge for what he had done. Instead, we got a behind closed doors father and son scolding from the Major. With that scolding came the first "thank you" for what we had done for our country. The Major spent some quality time (off the record) with us. Along with the praise, he also issued warnings of misguided civilians at home and advice on how to give ourselves the time to adjust back into civilian life.

The Major's words were the first (and only) kind, caring ones received throughout the discharge process in Pleiku. The E-6 got a purple heart for being an asshole in the line of duty. I'm kidding of course.

The next day I was off to Cam Ranh Bay for more paperwork. On our way back to our barracks I saw what appeared to be an Olympic sized swimming pool. I rubbed my eyes in disbelief. It was no dream. I chowed down at the mess hall, grabbed my towel, and off I went. It was a huge pool with deck chairs all around it. I was totally alone (which was a state I had come to be accustomed to). The sun was still high in the sky, so I thought I would get a nice red face and tanned up body to show off to my family and friends when I got home in three days.

The water was cool and crystal clear, so I swam until I was exhausted. Then I fell asleep on the deck lounger and jumped in again after I woke up. The cool water took the sting off my sunburned body - just like it used to do at the lake back home. I was in disbelief of what was happening to me, but right then I didn't care about anything. It was a true Selah moment in time!

I went from dosing off and ultimately fell into a deep sleep. Right about then a "thump, thump, thump" woke me up and then the sirens totally destroyed my Miami Beach Holiday.

"Holy shit!" I thought as I grabbed my towel and ran toward my barracks.

For a second, I forgot where my barracks was, then I thought, "What difference does it make where my barracks is?" - any barracks will do.

I quickly remembered that I had turned in all my weapons. "God damn it!"

There were deep drainage ditches on either side of the road and the red clay which formed them was slippery and smooth. I fell into one of the ditches while taking a short cut to the closest building I could see. I was on my hands and knees, crawling up to ground level when the mortars started to impact. I let myself slip down to the bottom of the red clay ditch. The ditch was a custom made gift from above that allowed me to miss all of the ground level shrapnel.

A few more rounds and it was over. So there I was in my shorts and combat boots - covered with red mud. I had my faithful green towel, but I was unable to get out of the ditch. It was dark now and there wasn't another soul in sight or within earshot.

Just when I thought I had seen and experienced it all, now it appeared I was going to spend the night in a fucking ditch, without a weapon.

The bugs were now eating me alive and my only defense was a green towel to cover my sunburned body. I could write a book about green towels. I walked for 10 minutes in order to find a spot where the ditch leveled out with the road and enabled me to get out.

I provided a good laugh for a bunch of GI's on my walk back to the barracks. That night I was laughing at myself during my shower and right up to the time I dosed off for my last night in Pleiku.

Somehow, Cam Ranh Bay retained its' "Jewel of the Orient" status for the duration of the war. The same was true during WWII when many buildings were spared from the relentless bombings in England and Germany. There is another book on that phenomenon too.

Due to the advancement in technology where bombing can be executed with pin-point accuracy, the wars in Iraq and Afghanistan spared the lives of countless civilians, but not so in Nam.

Maybe both sides of the war in Vietnam knew, in the back of their minds, that one day it would be over and the tourists would once again return to this paradise of the Far East - so why fuck it up?

Well, for me, it was one of the giant steps on my journey back to Buffalo. It held the unique distinction of being the only place in the whole country that I was looking forward to seeing once again.

The walkways of white sand in between buildings that I remembered from one year ago had changed into wooden plank paths. They were crude, but neatly elevated sidewalks with an ample amount of signs to identify the names of buildings and directions to wherever you needed to go. Like visiting an old friend in a strange, out of town hospital, I noticed the changes and similarities - as every step I took was a further departure from the familiar hospital I once knew back home.

Once out of the city of Pleiku's firebase in the central highlands, the treatment I received was noticeably different (and welcomed).

I felt the appreciation in their words and the empathy from their hearts was bigger than Dallas. It was welcomed by us all from the time we disembarked my last flight in a C-130 to when they bused me out to the tarmac where that beautiful Pan Am 707 was waiting to take us home.

This was the place where I got to see the Bob Hope show with Rachel Welch, Joey Bishop and the Dallas Cowboy Cheerleaders. Now it was the place where the final curtain would fall on the most significant command performance of my life.

All of the buildings where we did our paperwork and received our final paychecks were air conditioned. The medical facilities were spotless, the mess halls like restaurants, and the NCO Club reminded me of the fancy joints I would take my best girlfriend back home.

On the night before I left country, I went to the NCO Club for a few beers and met a young, very pretty "Donut Dolly" who just got into country. She quit college to come to Vietnam. These girls volunteered to travel everywhere in country, to various firebases and outposts just to fill a sandbag with a GI who hadn't seen an American woman in months. They would simply walk around your hill, smile, and say 'Hi" or talk for a minute and move on to the next guy. They'd give you a line like, "I want you to know that we appreciate you back home and I want you to know that I think you're great!"

My Dolly and I walked out of the NCO Club and onto a large deck overlooking the bay (which was as calm and flat as a lake!) The moon was full and the steel guitar was flooding the air with sounds it had never heard before. We tried to hold on to this awkward moment without knowing how.

She had short, dark brown hair and lots of freckles. She wanted to know everything about my year in the boonies.

I started a dozen times and gave up trying to complete a sentence. She saw my struggle and just calmly said, "It's okay, let's talk about some other things."

She wore a blue and white seersucker dress with a dark blue belt around her waist. There were blue buttons in the front which went all the way up to the small collar around her neck. I told her I really liked her dress and asked her to please take it off so we could make love for the rest of the night.

She laughed out of control and told me there would be plenty of that when I got home.

We recounted our childhood experiences and told stories about when we were in school and times with our families back home. We talked for hours on end.

I was a little drunk by 1:00 am when we decided to say good night. I gave her a hug and a quick kiss. That's when I decided to verbalize a few warnings to her. It was more like a father-daughter talk (which sobered me up for a brief moment). I cried a little - which surprised her (and me too).

My words were emanating from a place that I didn't think existed in me anymore. It was a mystery to me where all this came from.

My thoughts were a precursor of who I was about to become. They were the nebulous bits and pieces of who I was to be in the future after a year of hammering my character on the anvil of Vietnam. It still remains a mystery to me why I talked to her that way.

Einstein once said, "The most beautiful thing we can experience is the mysterious. It is the source of all art and science. He to whom this emotion is stranger, who can no longer pause to wonder and stand rapt in awe, is as good as dead; his eyes are closed."

My conscious awareness was not connecting the dots of my life. My little Donut Dolly was a sneak preview before the main feature started. This was starting to resemble "The Lady or the Tiger," which I read in high school. I was afraid to choose.

I knew I was not dead because my eyes were open, but that was all I was sure of. I was coming out of a coma and I was astonished that my responses were not what they used to be. Vietnam's grip was strong and deep in me.

"Why did I say that?" and "What made me do that?" were the questions arising in my head - and I was not even home yet. Thank God for Jack Daniels!

My flight home was scheduled for the next day. Having misplaced my frame of reference for thoughts like "the next day," caused me to sleep several inches above my cot that night (in spite of the beer).

The processing buildings seemed to be open day and night, leaving you with the option of going wherever you needed to go, whenever you wanted to go.

So I rose with the sun and picked up my summer dress uniform, new boots, and the medals and ropes that I would wear on my starched shirt as I prepared for traveling home. I dropped off all my shit (as we called it) in the barracks and headed over to the showers with all my money and one green towel. There is definitely something to be said about green towels in Vietnam.

In the Army, you sleep in strange places with new faces all the time, so you put your money in your hand then put a sock on your hand, pulling it up to your elbow. Then you use your hand as a pillow when you sleep. That is, of course, if you want to have any money in your pocket the next day. It's a long time in between paydays (which were once a month), so you learned how to hold onto your money in more ways than one.

It was a short walk on the wooden planks to the latrines and shower complex. There were actual toilets made of porcelain and white sinks with chrome faucets. I thought they had stopped making them. This was a warning sign; thinking how foreign a normal bathroom fixture appeared. I put my cash in a plastic bag and took it with me into the shower. I washed my hair and rinsed it over and over again until the reddish rinse water turned to a kind of orange yuckiness.

It actually took months to get my scalp clean after I got home, but this was at least a beginning. The soapy wash cloth was stinging me as it discovered all the unattended sores, mostly on my ass, from not being able to bathe for a year.

It was one of the most refreshing showers of my life, next to the one I had with my Irish girlfriend, D, in the Drake

Hotel in San Francisco just before leaving for Nam. The particulars of that steamy shower might be in my next book.

By the time I got back to my barracks, I was ringing wet in sweat from the insane heat and humidity.

I packed my duffle bag, picked up my 201 file (which we were told to guard with our life), and bought two packs of Camels.

I was down to three hours (which used to seem like three days in a firefight), but now felt more like three minutes as the clock was actually speeding up for the first time in 1968.

They bused us out to the tarmac where a highly polished aluminum Pan Am Boeing 707, which was being topped off with fuel, sat next to a B-52 bomber that was being loaded with bombs. The wings of the B-52 stretched so far from the fuselage that poles with wheels on them had to be placed at the tips of the wings to relieve the pressure on the welds and superstructure of the plane. The top of the plane was painted an ominous black-gray-blue sort of night color which met a cloud-like milky, white on the bottom in waves that eased into each other wherever the spray gun wanted to go.

I remembered reading about what happened to Lot's wife as she walked away from Sodom and Gomorra, so as I walked up the long staircase through the entrance of my silver bird, I did not look back - a symbolic, feeble attempt to sever my past from my future. Lot's wife succumbed to the addiction of permitting her past to steer her future. She had the opportunity to change and better her life, but due to her lack of identity, faith and self-esteem (which couldn't be shaped or altered by mere circumstances) she was transformed into a pillar of salt. What we DO does not define who we ARE!

I recently rekindled some relationships with my high school classmates after missing our 50 year reunion. They all thought I died in Vietnam. One of my friends, M, whom I hadn't seen or heard from in 53 years lives in Florida, so we got together over dirty martinis. She's been through 3 husbands, kids, grandkids, etc... I've had two marriages, half a dozen careers, bouts with booze, yada, yada... She told me I was the exact same Kenny she knew in 8th grade. I felt the same about her. At 12 years old, we had a little thing for each other, so now we're doing something about it. Neither of us are looking back. Vietnam or no Vietnam, it's not healthy to look back.

As I entered the plane, the two most beautiful women in the world were smiling right at me. I was greeted with a handshake and their hands were as cold as ice from being in the air-conditioned cabin. The inside of the plane was more like a meat locker, but nobody was complaining.

Everyone was either smiling or crying. I saw in a movie how Japanese people cry when they are happy, but this was no movie.

We buckled up during a short taxi to the runway. We stopped for just a minute, then we heard the roar of the engines cranking up while the brakes were pushing the nose of the plane down with a slight bounce. I glanced out the window at the flaps as they adjusted into position along with the sounds of all the hundreds of motors in the wings

234

pushing and pulling. Then the brakes were released as we went to full throttle. The G force was pushing us into the seats and the bumps on the runway were smoothing out and getting farther apart when the nose lifted up and the back wheels left the runway. The sound of the motors folding up the landing gears started up, but were dwarfed and drowned out by the roar inside the cabin. The cheering sounded like a bases loaded home run at the World Series or the winning touchdown catch in the last 5 seconds of a Super Bowl. Everyone was crying by this time, including the hostesses. Then came the liquor carts, one after another.

The hot food was delicious and the sandwiches and snacks never stopped. The drinks were either dirt cheap or free - I really cannot remember. There were poker games breaking out everywhere since we all had pockets full of money. After 3 hours in the air celebrating, we transitioned into an airborne Las Vegas. The crew members would take a break and join in the fun. Some of the guys chose just to sleep through it all - and that was okay too.

We stopped on the Island of Guam for fuel and then continued on to Fort Lewis, Washington.

A few guys got sick from drinking too much - and practically all of us were sleeping by the time we got into the tail end of our nine hour flight.

I had forgotten how horrible the weather is in the state of Washington in December, but then why should I remember?

It was either raining snowflakes or the snow was turning into rain as it hit my sunburned skin. The wind was ferocious as it pulled door knobs out of your wet hands and blew through the jammed open windows of the buildings. We were herded again like cattle in the middle of the night. Now this was the Army I was used to. They were processing GI's day and night, so nothing ever closed.

I had lost 100% of my hearing in my left ear, leaving me with a distinct disadvantage when it came to understanding directions over all the chaos of 75 people coming and 75 going out of one room at the same time.

Some of the hinges on the swinging doors that lead into the shower rooms were broken, so the steam from the hot water inside met the outside 25 degree temperature, making clouds that drifted down to the sidewalk and onto the street. This made us all wonder what the hell was going on in there as we approached.

The idea was to give all the filthy grunts a shower and a steak dinner as a welcome home gesture. This is all taking place at 1:00 am (which made no difference to those in charge). If the Army said everyone gets a steak for your first meal, you will get a steak - day or night, well done, medium, or rare - want it or not, you WILL eat your fucking steak and like it.

The Army was processing huge numbers of people every day, all day. People were being processed either going to Vietnam or returning from Vietnam. You ended up feeling like a pig going to be slaughtered or a cow pushed off a truck into a grazing pasture.

Evidently, the Generals who came up with the concept of brainwashing us and de-humanizing our enemy also created the plans for the homecoming for those of us who could walk.

For three days we were screamed at, threatened and herded with statements like:

"You WILL be at so and so building by 1300 hours or else you will be detained for an undetermined amount of time until the following incoming personnel have processed. Building "K's" shipments of personnel from the previous buildings load of buildings R's overflow roster. It would behoove you all to adhere to the following dates and times for departing flights to various cities. The cadre of this facility are not, I repeat, are not responsible for your prompt arrival at gates of departure. Schedules of all flights are posted on the bulletin boards of your assigned temporary quarters, BUT they are subject to hourly cancelations and/or changes. If, for reasons of neglect, you miss your flight, your two week leave time will be cut accordingly. And if... and on and on!"

Of course it was always a PFC, who just got in the Army, doing the announcing over the roar of 40 or 50 GI's shouting, "What the fuck did he say, man? Hey, speak up asshole!"

This situation was tougher than Vietnam!

I have no clue how I survived Ft. Lewis, Washington, but I did. I was successfully custom fitted for my tailored dress greens. Then I ate my steak, received a physical exam, and of course, filled out a little more paperwork. All this happened in three days - which equaled, in terms of stress, any three days spent in the jungles of the central highlands.

I picked up my boarding pass to Buffalo, New York and vowed to never again return to the northwest corner of the United States of America.

I called Mom and Dad to tell them what time I would arrive. I got on board the plane, heading to Chicago for a four hour layover and then arriving home sweet home at 9:30pm.

In order to fulfill my two year obligation to the Army, I had five more months to serve on an active duty assignment at Fort Hood, Texas. But not yet, for right now, I only had room to think about home.

We landed at O'Hare field to fuel up and pick up passengers, so I decided to visit a watering hole on the concourse - which, luckily for me, was close to my gate. It was a small horseshoe bar filled with businessmen in suits and a group of football players. I was the only uniformed dude in the bar and there was just one stool available. I ordered a 7 Crown and water with a twist of lemon. The guy next to me said, "That's on me, bartender."

Three hours later they poured me back on the plane. Every person in that bar had a kind word for me and tears in their eyes as we spoke. I didn't want to, nor was able to, share any of the horrific details of Vietnam with them; respectfully, no one asked. Without giving it much thought at the time, that unwillingness stayed with me for many years to follow.

I had a few more drinks on the plane during the short flight to Buffalo. A drop dead gorgeous airline hostess reluctantly served me more booze, but then again, every woman I saw was gorgeous. She kept saying, "Are you sure you want another drink soldier? Maybe you've had enough?"

In spite of the numbness from the 7 Crown, my mind was drifting back to my buddies in Nam who were probably being dropped off on a CA or humping just another hill while waiting for the AK-47's to break the silence of a rainy afternoon. How ironic it was that I should be here and they should be there. I felt guilty for not staying.

It was snowing when I got off the plane, but then in Buffalo, it's always snowing. I staggered down the steps as the bitter cold temperature sobered me up a bit. I got down on my hands and knees and gave Buffalo a big kiss as I tasted the icy asphalt. Mom and Dad were there. As I stood next to them, we tried our best to verbalize our feelings in words - finding it impossible, we just cried and hugged. I totally enjoyed the ride home in a blizzard of record proportion while slipping and sliding down Genesee Street to Bailey Ave, then Ferry St, and finally Wyoming Ave. I remembered the way to get home, but was in the dark about coming back.

The kinetic energy of my physical and mental movement resembled a cue ball that hits the rack so hard it bounces backwards on impact and then goes forward again, hitting the lead ball, sending all the others everywhere on the table.

A scattering was going to take place. Like random balls in the rack, none of my friends had any idea where they would wind up after being hit by me - and neither did I, after introducing them to the new me.

When we arrived home, Mom, Dad and I had sandwiches and talked for hours at the dining room table. Every now and then my Mom would look at Dad and her eyes would roll up as he would respond to me with a "What can we do?" look on his face. They communicated between themselves in this weird non-verbal exchange as if I was not aware of it taking place. The only things that made sense that night were the shots and beers.

My first life with all the people I knew ended when I arrived in Vietnam. Now I was on a collision course with my new life without a requiem for those I had just left behind.

Sitting there at that dining room table, I knew that no one would ever understand what I had done or what my year was like, so I decided, right there, right then, to never try explaining.

My Dad and I got wasted that night and I slept through most of the next day.

Dad had some good friends in the car business, and I needed one, so he took me out to the lot where he used to work to see about getting me a nice Chevy.

We were talking a mile a minute on the way to the car dealership as I looked into the rear view mirror. On the bottom of the glass was a warning sticker that read, "Objects in the rear are closer than they appear." The innocuous warning sent me back to the boonies quicker than Scotty beaming Captain Kirk back up to the Enterprise.

My Dad wondered why I stopped talking and suddenly got a little distant. He didn't know how to handle his son, but neither did I. I was being introduced to my new life - and adapting to things like jumping out of my skin when a car backfires, shutting down at the smell of forest fires, and insisting on sitting facing the entrance door of every restaurant I go to for the rest of my life. This was just not going to be fun.

The booze, which shut down the ever-advancing past for a few hours, was the only relief I could get, so the daily ratio of hours of sobriety to being drunk were weighing heavily on the 7 Crown side.

The expectations of my family and friends were evidenced in their actions. They didn't know how to treat me - and I felt it. They all loved me and honored me for what I had done for our country, but deep down they were in fear that the effects of what I had done had permanently changed the Ken of old into the stranger they were talking to. I could see they were a little afraid of the Ken I had become.

There was a mutual uneasiness from my perspective as well. Everyone was acting as if I had spent a year in rehab for some kind of addiction; not knowing how to reconnect with the old Ken.

I thought I had a contagious disease because people did not want to hug me (except my Mom). Handshakes were offered, but they were the arm extended ones - not firm and warm, with eye contact and a smile, as they used to be.

I was the new dog in the kennel and my two week leave was becoming a pain in the ass with everyone sniffing my behind.

I didn't know how to be nice any more than I didn't know how to shoot human beings before I went to Nam. I just wished I could sit down with my Grandma and snuggle those pieces into the puzzle while seeing the big picture develop. But she had died, leaving me a little more alone.

In 1999, my Dad passed away, 31 years after my tour in Nam. I did not shed a tear. I loved my Dad desperately, but I could not cry. In 2000 my Mom died, I didn't shed a tear. In 2007 my wife of 38 years died. I cried one time, by myself, in the living room the morning after for 10 minutes - and that was it. No more, no less. My wife always said I was as cold as ice. I scared her when I just went to bed and slept after my parents died. I had become a fish.

I had only been home two days. Now I could not wait to leave what I almost died for and dreamt about. I just could not fit back in at home. Buffalo moved away without a forwarding address.

I felt like my life had been reduced to my expired driver's license and my desire for only two things: to get drunk and laid, but not necessarily in that order.

I made a vow to myself and to God in 1967. I made a deal with Him when I got in country. I said, "I'll tell you what God, I won't fuck any women over here, and you know I love women, and you get me home safe and sound." "After all," I said to myself, "I came here to shoot people, not make love to them, so how about that God?"

I don't believe in vows now and I didn't believe in them back then, but I wanted to. So I cut my little deal - and who knows? We all make deals with ourselves and that may sound stupid, but I did it. Well I'm writing this book, so...!

By the time I got home, I was a volcano ready to erupt. After twelve days, I was more exhausted from sex than coming back from Nam. I took my sore penis to Texas for 5 more months of active duty at Fort Hood.

I really could not figure out any of this bullshit, so getting back into uniform was a relief. My buddies were as confused as I was, but the stars at night were big and bright, deep in the heart of Texas - and there were lots of beer joints.

John Donne penned with unique clarity:

> *No man is an island,*
> *Entire of itself,*
> *Every man is a piece of the continent,*
> *A part of the main.*
> *If a clod be washed away by the sea,*
> *Europe is less.*
> *As well as if a promontory were*
> *As well as if a manor of thy friends,*
> *Or of then own were.*
> *Any man's death diminishes me,*
> *Because I am involved in mankind,*
> *And therefore never send to know for*
> *Whom the bell tolls,*
> *It tolls for thee.*

I know now it was naïve of me to expect my life to pick up where it left off, but we all play the melancholy game of reminiscing about when pork chops were 10 cents a pound and you could buy a new car for $1,000.00. "Those were the days..." sang Archie and Edith.

Proverbs says, "Hope deferred makes the heart sick" and that's where I was, in a nutshell. There was no going back and I knew it, but I wanted to.

Stateside military duty was a whole different ball of wax, as I was to discover.

The kettle drums were sounding a long, anticipated crescendo of my brief two year career in the Army. What should have been a date to joyfully look forward to, was now a declivous mountainside peppered with rocks and trees.

In Vietnam, we feared the unseen punji stakes and booby traps. In the states, the things I could see made me fearful.

Much to my amazement, I landed an exceptionally cushy job for my last five months.

In Vietnam, the Army had a need of professional career people such as dentists, doctors, CPA's, attorneys, etc... and they were kept in rear areas which were relatively safe and secured.

It was not required for these people to go through boot camp or the type of training needed to actually do any fighting. They did, however, need to at least be acquainted with the weapons that were being used and have some knowledge as to how they worked, just in case.

My job was to show the doctors how to load and fire an M-16, or teach an attorney how to throw a hand grenade, etc...

The Army gave us 17 days to prepare them to work in a combat zone, which seemed like a reasonable amount of time, until the long awaited end of the first day of training.

It was laid out to be an informal get together - and it was. We wore the patches of the units we were assigned to in Vietnam.

They had already received their orders and knew where they were headed in country; therefore, they recognized the patches we wore as their new home. So we formed some groups of four or five and talked about everything. They asked us whatever they wanted to and we familiarized them with what to expect, having been there and bought the t-shirt.

I took my group to the hand grenade pit and gave them a demonstration of how to pull the pin, hold the spoon tight to the ball, and then throw it like a football over the top edge. I then showed them how to quickly duck their heads down and face the opposite direction before it detonated.

I told them that the hand grenades were the impact detonation type, which didn't give your enemy an opportunity to throw it back to you within so many seconds.

Everyone was to throw a dud grenade for practice, then a live one. I threw first - going through it by the numbers to get them accustomed to the sound of the impact and the shrapnel whistling over their heads at ground level. Then I did it again - assuming that college educated folks possessed an above average level of intelligence. After all, so I mistakenly thought, this was not rocket science. The instructions were few and quite clear and simple.

I noticed the obtuse expression on the Doctor's face (which is a normal reaction to holding the power to inflict death in your hand). But what's the difference between a grenade and a scalpel, I thought.

There were only the two of us in the pit - just in case there was an accident. Doc threw the dud grenade without a hitch. I handed him the live one and he started to shake. He pulled the pin, activating the firing device, then switched the grenade from one hand to the other while holding the spoon down. I hollered at him to not do that - it was a tricky move even for a seasoned warrior. Now I started shaking. I did not want to upset him further, but told him not to do that. I simply told him to throw it out of our pit. He ignored my command, switching hands again.

I then grabbed the grenade out of his hand while holding the spoon and threw it out of our pit of horror. I pulled him down and pushed his face in the dirt. My next thought was to kick his ass, but I settled for calling him the stupidest son of a bitch I ever met - following that by shouting at the top of my lungs "Get the fuck out of my pit, asshole!" I then waited for them to send in the next dumb mother fucker.

All of these people were Captains or higher in rank, so I could have been court marshaled for my behavior, but I didn't care.

I decided to climb out of the pit and give them the most important piece of life saving knowledge they would need in Vietnam.

I told them, "Get accustomed to being talked to the way I hollered at the Doc, because in Vietnam, rank does not count for shit. However stupid counts, and it will send you home in a fucking body bag. Let this be a wakeup call for you all."

Then I told them the stories of the E-5 teacher I had at Fort Polk in the claymore class who saved my life more than once - and you guessed it, I gave them the infamous line "When someone tells you to do something, DO IT, don't think!!!"

I then apologized for my language, but it wasn't necessary. The Doctor thanked me for saving his life with tears in his eyes, and we all became good friends.

My two year marriage to the Army had a singular purpose, which was to shoot people. Training professionals wasn't fitting in and all of this just added to my already confused state of mind.

I calmed down in order to survive the next five months (which was a tactical adjustment I was used to doing). Getting rid of the four letter expletives was definitely necessary. Next in order was applying "that chameleon thing" to the rest of my social behavior skills.

I bought a 1955 Ford from a local car lot and settled down to an eight hour day of work - followed by evenings of pitchers of draft beer and really good Mexican food.

In the Book of Dzyan (BC 3000) it is written: "The causes of existence had been done away with; the visible that was, and the invisible that is, rested in eternal non-being - the one being."

Being surrounded by a Battalion of NVA seasoned warriors was less challenging than these professionals with room temperature IQ's who were incapable of handling the tools of war, but I had to make the best of it, so I did.

One of my girlfriends back home called to inform me that she was late. This news gave me the same feeling as when I got my draft notice; another out of control situation I could not change. I couldn't manage this with an M-16. Welcome to the real world.

My situations were adding up like compound interest.

Life was simple when your food was dropped down to you like manna from heaven. Every day you got your food and water - and your magic wand had an 18 round clip that everyone paid attention to with great respect.

It was not that I did not want a child, a wife and a home with a white picket fence and all that goes with it, "just not now," was my haunting thought.

Life was force-feeding me. It was like when I was eighteen months old, sitting in a highchair, and my mother was pushing in a spoonful of applesauce every time I opened my mouth, then sweeping all the excess off my cheeks with another spoonful to follow - and then another, and another, and....!

I thought about signing up for six more years, and then I thought about my thoughts. I abandoned that option like the black plague. Any course would be better than killing people for a living.

Ahhhh! If I made it through Vietnam, I'll make it through anything life has in store for me - so I thought!

I'll spare you the boring details of state-side military duty and fast forward to my final physical exam prior to my discharge.

The last three days were absorbed in reams of paperwork and a final physical exam (which was moving along nicely). Until, that is, when I got a message to report to the hospital to clear something up. It's not a good thing to get a message like that!

All of us stationed in the field suffered with some degree of hearing loss, not to mention the fungi issue showing up under our nails, in our intestines, and wherever moisture exists - one of the areas being in our ears.

As it turned out, the impact of that B-40 rocket on April 26th handed me a souvenir I would carry for life.

The E.N.T. doctor took note of a draining infection in my left ear during my exam and wanted to discuss my options. The eardrum had burst as a result of the explosion and the unattended infection had eaten its way dangerously close to my facial nerve. The Doc lost me with medical terminology as my head was nodding up and down saying, "Ah huh, ah huh!"

I just wanted to go home, and was thankful to return on my own two legs.

The Doc offered me a visit to Walter Reed to fix my situation with possible surgery. This meant I would have to extend my tour of active duty, which gave me a bad taste in my mouth.

My other option was to simply sign on the dotted line that I was made aware of the problem and then chose to be released from active duty.

I opted for the latter, and would later regret the decision. Yet there was a notation on my medical discharge form that a serious issue with my left ear did exist. It was made official by the initials of the Doctor, his name, and date.

Forty years later, that form which I kept intact and tucked away in my safety deposit box, proved to be the instrument that enabled me to receive a percentage of disability from the V.A. It was another lesson I learned from my Dad about keeping paperwork.

Shortly after being discharged, Blue Cross and Blue Shield took care of the bills for a radical mastoidectomy on my left ear. I was on the verge of facial paralysis and losing 100% of my hearing as a result of not taking care of it all sooner.

The infections were ongoing - along with the constant ringing and ear aches (which I'm experiencing right now as I write). Oh well! The most annoying aspect is the inability to have a conversation in a restaurant, especially with the waitress rapping off the special of the day. But worst of all, I cannot understand the lyrics of songs by anyone except Frank Sinatra.

After a while I grew weary of saying "Huh?" and "Pardon me?"

People think I am not paying attention. Nothing gets me more pissed off than being accused of having selective hearing. You cannot give people a half an hour explanation of why they have to speak up a little - and some folks just do not give a shit about you being in Vietnam because they did not agree with the war anyway.

So the Big Ben wind-up alarm clock that signaled my first day in the United States Army rang once again, twenty minutes early, to usher in the last day.

We drove back home to Buffalo in my buddies 1957 Chevy - never saying the first word about Vietnam. Every mile marker was another metaphorical shovel full of dirt that was filling in the grave of my life that ended in July of 1969.

I drifted back to those weird thoughts or impressions I had when I first got in country about "Being rewarded" or something to that effect. I could not remember, so I decided to just listen - again!

Chapter 16
In Retrospect

Coming to grips with internal chatter is a healthy exercise, but there are times when we find ourselves unable to even think. There is a scripture that relates to this condition. "As a man thinks in his heart, so is he"- Proverbs 23:7. Notice it does not say WHAT he thinks, but rather AS he thinks. So facts, as we traditionally consider them, are surprisingly not the actual motivating factors that are guiding our direction in life.

Where we find ourselves is a result of HOW we see things. Our perceptions are the molds or the shaping hands of life, not the events we experience. So if the scripture is correct, what we look at in the mirror is the product, or result, of HOW we look at ourselves.

More than anything, I remember listening to myself in Vietnam. I listened as an option when I first got in country - and on purpose before leaving. It's hard to hear when everyone is talking and it's impossible to understand when you can't hear yourself.

What we tell ourselves is what we really believe about who we are. Those who are awake pick up on all this stuff in casual conversation.

Paul Anka nailed it in the lyrics of Sinatra's greatest hit "My Way" when he sang "I ate up... and spit it out..." It's not what happens that cripples us, it's how we handle what happens. AND it's not simply the worn out, "get up after you fall" cliché either. Getting back up on the horse that threw you is important, but HOW we think about ourselves during the fall and process of getting back up is the real gist of the matter.

Experience is an excellent teacher when we learn to listen to our "self-talk." We become really good students when we own up to the self-sabotaging chatter; using defeats, shortcomings, failures and mistakes as tools to cut away the negativity we constantly subject ourselves to. I'm talking about the clutter that's wayyyyy down there.

A few years ago I hit my left thumb with a hammer while trying to straighten out a sheet metal elbow that was damaged during shipping. A huge blood blister erupted immediately. My thumb was throbbing with pain and blood was gushing everywhere as I swung my hand back and forth and grimaced from the pain. I noticed that the skin was intact on the top and bottom, but the sides were wide open, down to the bone. My work mates were ready to haul me to the hospital, but I decided not to go. I allowed it to bleed, thus cleaning the cuts. I applied a sterile Band-Aid and wrapped it with duct tape. I left it alone for a week and, to my surprise, both cuts had healed nicely. There was no infection, so I was left with two long scars and a slightly puffed up thumb to this day. What's the point?

Well, my tour in Nam as a grunt was exactly like my left thumb incident. I was drafted (which I consider an accident). It wasn't my choice. I stood idly by, watching the life leaking out of me. I was out of control, but I saw a healthy connection above and beneath me - considering my past and future. It was my decision to handle the problem. I'm not blaming anything or anybody for what happened to me.

Now I'm looking at a completely restored, fully functional life. I've got some scars and a little bubble of flesh on my left thumb that renders no pain.

The voices I hear today do not condemn me or make me feel guilty - nor do they tell me that I'm some special dude for choosing to go to Nam and fight for my country instead of moving to Canada to avoid the draft.

Navel gazing affords us limited perspectives. Too much time spent looking in the rear view mirror puts us on collision courses with our future.

Sure, there are scars, but the voices, ah the relentless voices that once spoke to me have transitioned to the calming sounds of ankle-high waves; which neither push me away nor draw me out to sea. One on top of another - devoid of condemnation or affirmation.

I am, however, one of the fortunate victims of the tragedy - or should I say, the accident of Vietnam. The truth about how and why it started will never be told - just the same as the Kennedy assassination. It may be best we don't know the real truth about the 60's.

1.4 million Vietnamese people died as compared to a little over 58,000 Americans. ACCIDENT may be a poor choice of words, but I'll bet you have an intersection in your town that has claimed the lives of countless people and you've wondered why. So perhaps it's not such a bad choice.

Armchair quarterbacks have consumed thousands of gallons of coffee at Starbucks while debating over the WHYS and WHEREFORES of Vietnam; while B-52 pilots and grunts like me wrestle with ourselves about the lives we personally brought to an end... and the beat goes on.

"Don't mean nothin'" does not work anymore for those of us who witnessed the horror, but "Think Snow" does - and remembering that innocent bumper sticker continues to lift me out the doldrums whenever I need it.

Maybe ignorance is bliss and maybe not knowing what really happened in the 60's is a good thing. Messing with peoples' lives is a complex issue - especially if one of your loved ones has to go. There is a need in all of us to point the blame at someone for the troubles, or accidents, or hard times, etc... The Doctor prescribed the wrong medication, so it's his fault. The other guy went through a red light, so it's his fault. Listen honey, you wanted the new car so now we cannot go on a vacation this year, so it's your fault.

Vietnam was someone's fault, but WHO? There was no doubt about the "who" in WW II, or Iraq and Afghanistan. Usually when the Hitler's, Saddam Hussein's, and Osama Bin Laden's die, the war is over. Or maybe we should be blaming a WHAT - like communism, al-Qaeda, or maybe oil, or...!

More coffee, please!

When I was a teenager, my dad bought me a tan colored cocker spaniel that I named "Taffy" (for obvious reasons). He was just a little puppy when I walked him down to the end of my block to a great delicatessen which sold the best penny candy in Buffalo.

The owners knew me well and I couldn't wait to show off my new dog. What I did not know was that they owned a cat which just had a litter of kittens. As soon as the bell rang over the door announcing our arrival the cat attacked my puppy, tearing him up badly. Blood was everywhere and it all belonged to my pup. I kicked the cat, breaking something in her body, but she would not quit attacking my dog and now me too. She bit my leg, sinking her eye teeth into my calf and then she hung on like a pit bull.

The store owners were screaming at me to leave, but the cat would not let go. I reached down, pulling the cat off me and I threw her into the candy case, breaking the glass and cutting her all up. She bled to death in an ocean of penny candy - and we ran out of the store.

THE VIETNAMESE PEOPLE WERE PROTECTING THEMSELVES FROM AN INVASION THAT WAS THREATENING THEIR LIVES AND FUTURE EXISTENCE.

You know, maybe those store keepers should have posted a sign saying NO DOGS ALLOWED! And maybe Congress should have put their foot down, saying NO to the President who sent the first troops in after DIEN BIEN FU. And maybe that husband should have said NO to his wife about buying that new car!

I still have the scars on my leg from that damn cat, but my dog died decades ago. Now I don't care much about Vietnam anymore or why I went into that candy store on that day - so why not join me and "Think a little Snow?"

Chapter 17
Ulanni

Thank you for taking the time to read this book about me and my experiences in Vietnam. It has been a one-sided communication because you have found out much more about me than I will ever get to know about you.

I was advised to not be concerned or worry about what you, the reader, think of me, but I do. For whatever it's worth, I do want you to know that efforts to eschew my acrimonious observations took a back seat to my desire for being a shade different in the publishing of this work by sharing the contents of my heart without reservation; rather than to follow some of the traditional writings about the war in Vietnam that preceded mine.

If nothing else, being a combat infantry man forcibly taught me the masterful art of the state of loneliness.

Confronting our enemies in the journeys of life happen when our heads hit the pillow and we cannot avoid confrontations or escape from them - like when we join the rank and file of a local Union or the Country Club in our gated sub-division. There exists no security in numbers when facing the battles of life. And it is my conviction after personal experience that Carl Jung, Alfred Adler, and Freud barely scratched the surface in the science of our complex make up - not to mention the endless stream of religious zealots on TV who have all the answers to everything in life.

Commander Perry's statement, "We have met the enemy and he is us," is more than apropos.

There will always be wars and rumors of war. There will always be those who start them, those who fight in them, finish them, and of course, lose them and die because of them.

We were an army of lions in Vietnam, being led by lambs. The pride that I was honored to serve with were willing to lay down their lives for the country they loved and I witnessed many who did just that - some in my arms.

I'm still waiting for the day that is void of a thought about Vietnam - one 24 hour span of time that's not hooked to the jungles of Southeast Asia.

For me, my experience in the Army was a closely guarded, invisible handicap - until now.

Combat Veterans learn to adapt to the losses of limbs, sight, vital organs and a host of other physical infirmities that we come back with after war. Yet the common threads running through the inside of all combat veterans are the things the world around us does not see. They are the wounds that can cripple the most.

No, I never have a day of complete freedom - and probably never will. It's because it's never over for us who went. I have adapted, however, turning it into a quasi-good thing because it places a demand on me to search for that day; even if it does not exist.

For all warriors there is a war after the war is over. Make no mistake, issuing an order is not the same as pulling the trigger. It would require me to write another book to explain the difference.

Some of us surrendered to a bottle, or an overdose, or living under bridges or behind bars; unable to keep a steady job or simply stop the paranoia of looking from side to side in a crowd.

You can Google the numbers yourself of incarcerations, suicides and divorce - and your computer will hear you say, "Oh my God!"

One of the "rewards" I wondered about on that strange day in Nam came in the form of a woman named Judy (who put up with me for 38 years). She said I was a kind man - imagine that!

Judy fought with me (and for me) and believed in me more than I believed in myself. I would not be here today if not for her.

She gave birth to Kim and Dave who are blessings in my life and were a joy to raise (except for a few times when...)!

I made them walk through my mine fields and was not an easy person to live with - especially in the beginning of our marriage. I drafted them into my personal war of hell that I carried with me wherever I went.

So Judy and I were on a visit to Phoenix to visit my son and his family. They have three great children, the oldest of whom is named Ulanni. We visited during the Christmas holidays - she was about eight years old at the time.

Ulanni signed up for a two day workshop project to make a mask out of newspaper using flour, water and a rubber band to hold it tight to your face. Normally, mom would be involved, but I volunteered to take my granddaughter. Ulanni was ecstatic about spending two whole days with Papa - and so was I.

Within the first hour, we were covered with glue from head to toe, creating a bond we both wanted. We got silly and laughed so much the director had to calm us down.

We went on a lunch break at 12:00, taking our snacks over to a bench facing a wall of glass where we could enjoy the flower beds and perfectly groomed hedges. Ulanni got a Butterfinger candy bar because they were Grandma's favorite, so she informed me (as if I didn't know), so we had to buy one for her before we went home.

Little did either of us know, Grandma would pass away in the seventh month of that year, 2007. When we finished eating, Ulanni told me that her dad told her that I was in the Army a long time ago and had to go to war way far away in a country named Vietnam.

"Oh really," I replied with a slightly reserved tone in my voice.

Then she asked me, "Why are there wars, and why did you have to go, Papa?"

I was blown away by her questions - and still am. I took a big bite of my candy bar, hoping the sugar would enlighten me and give me a minute to think.

How do you explain to an eight year old why it's okay to kill people?

Our two children knew I had gone to Vietnam, but were afraid to ask me anything about it when they were little kids for fear of having their heads chopped off. The war in Vietnam and my role there was a carefully guarded secret. I could not force myself to talk about it without knowing why I allowed my tour to become a taboo topic.

I ordered them to never look at my pictures from Nam and simply told them that I did not want to talk about the subject - ever!

Now I've got my grandchild beating on the same door. There was nowhere for me to hide this time. I had to open up about what I believed was true down deep in my heart - or at least try. I could not play escape and evasion - not with her, or not with myself anymore.

I caught myself speaking to her as if she were a two year old (which she astutely picked up on). She telegraphed her displeasure by concentrating on her candy bar. Ulanni is wise beyond her years, so she was respectful in her demeanor, and at the same time, knew I was camouflaging the truth, thinking she was too young to handle it.

I made a quantum leap by realizing it was not a little girl I was responding to, but rather myself!

She read my mind and said, "That's okay Papa, you don't have to talk about it."

I thought, I do not believe this; how could she be so smart? She's only eight! Is this what everyone has been seeing in me for 43 years?

So why did I go? Why does anyone go?

So I looked her right in the eye and started talking to myself. She took a drink of water, put down her candy bar and riveted her attention to my every word.

"Ulanni, some people in this world are mean."

"I know that," she answered.

"At school, huh?"

"Yep."

"Well, sometimes mean kids grow up to become mean adults, okay? And sometimes these mean adults get together into big groups, okay?"

"And these people want everything to go their way, like some of the kids at my school, Papa?"

"Yep, exactly. Have you seen those kids get into fights?"

"Yep, I have."

"Well, when those kids grow up, they have to stop fighting"

"I see," she nodded.

"But Ulanni, some people never grow up - and instead of fighting, they kill people if they don't get their way."

"I see." So the good people who grow up try to talk to the mean people. Okay, I see, but if the mean people will not listen and they kill people to get their way - well then they have to be stopped by good people. And sometimes they even have to be killed because they refuse to change. Oh, I see, and did you have to kill those mean people to make 'em stop?"

"Yeah, I did!"

"Okay, I see. Can we go home now, Papa?"

"Sure, let's stop and get a pizza on the way."

"Oh great, I love pizza - and so does Grandma!"

Do I dare end it like this? The truth is that there is no reality in life – only perception. The most complex dilemmas that occur during our allotted time on earth can be resolved with very simple solutions. How did an 8 year old girl accomplish what Harvard and Yale's finest stumble through with their leather couch techniques? I think we waste precious time with the feints in our lives, not discerning the mendacity that surrounds us all in our journey. My new imperative is: Live as if you were living for the second time and had acted as wrongly the first time as you are about to act now.

THE END

Or is it just the beginning?

About the Author

Ken Kinsler was born and raised in snowy Buffalo, New York. At the age of 26, his career as a sheet metal worker was interrupted by a draft notice from the US Army. Like thousands of other men, Ken found his life turned upside down and forever changed by an untimely and uninvited trip to Vietnam. The hardships he experienced and the friendships he formed during his tour of duty in a foreign war would forever change his life and his view of the world. His "return to normalcy" yielded a 38 year long marriage, two wonderful children and grandchildren.

Like many of his comrades in the war, Ken harbored thoughts and feelings from 1968, but chose to keep them to himself.

Later in life, Ken became a widower and an empty-nester. His enjoyment of retirement and his life in sunny Ormond Beach, Florida was trumped by the ever present thoughts of Vietnam.

No amount of counseling, introspective thought or rationalization could quell the firefight that was still raging inside him, 40 years after the fact. His pent-up emotions ultimately became the fuel and fodder for writing and publishing his first book about his Vietnam experience.

It is his hope that this book will be a "helping hand" that will land in the hands of soldiers who are about to deploy - or veterans who are grappling with the same demons that consumed him for over four decades.

FRIENDS OF COLOR

I'm holding a Browning automatic rifle — very heavy and very effective.

These are M.I.K.E Force Soldiers mentioned on page 125. M.I.K.E. represented (Mobile Strike Force Command) and they were trained through the C.I.D.G's (Civilian Irregular Defense Group). The C.I.D.G's program was created under the M.A.A.C.V (Military Assistance Command Vietnam), which took place from July 1963 - May 1965.

The 5th Special Forces Group (airborne) were assigned to the task for the entire operation based in Nha Trang.

What lush green jungle looked like after an application of
Agent Orange. (Page 19)

Our 4-Deuce mortars provided great night illuminations and pin-point devastation to poor ole' Charlie.

This daytime Convoy turned into the night time event
described on page 51.

The happy pregnant girl. (Page 55)

Our 105 Howiters could be towed by a jeep or dropped by parachute. Very accurate and deadly with a range of approximately 12,325 yds. (Page 88)

Kids are kids, no matter what's going on.

One of the T.O.C.S. (Battalion Tactical Operations Center)
I was assigned to, as mentioned on page 152.

My Black Beret came from a South Vietnamese Ranger in the B.D.Q. (Biet Dong Quan). They were trained by our Green Beret Special Forces in the early 1960's.

Best. Bath. Ever. (Page 67)

It was not unusual to see statues of the Prime Minister,
Charles De Galle. (Page 83)

The infamous open field peppered with tall trees.
(Page 165)

A typical C.A. (Combat Assault). The ground here was
completely drenched in Agent Orange.

These are my knees.

277

The late afternoon burial of my Viet Cong friend. R.I.P.
(Complete story on page 30)

A little puppy love.

When I took the point, I liked to put my "Pot" on backwards which afforded clearer vision to the thick tree tops.

This was the scene (described in Chapter 3). The fire base is in the foreground with all the antennas. The road to the summit is on the left - where I drove the Jeep.

One of our visits from a "Donut Dollie!" Oh, Happy Day!

Coming Home. Last Stop Cam Ranh Bay.

THINK SNOW.

Acknowledgements

A very special thanks to the following people who helped this book come to life:

- ➤ Many thanks to the management and staff of the V.A. facilities in Gainesville, Lake City, Orlando and Daytona Beach, Florida for all of their kindness, caring and professionalism.
- ➤ A special huge thank you to Dr. Noce at the Daytona Beach mental health clinic – without his help, I would not have been able to write this book.
- ➤ Art Direction and Creative Directors: David Kinsler, dkmedia, LLC. / Phoenix and Los Angeles - and Matt Ramey, BLACK TDA. / Los Angeles.
- ➤ Sean Donovan of SeanDon.com – editor, writing coach and publishing consultant.
- ➤ Special thanks to Linda Jimeian for typing and editing the original hand written legal pad manuscript.
- ➤ Kim Wiley, Maria Buscani and Al Donovan for proofreading.

Made in the USA
Charleston, SC
14 May 2015